THEY ALL LAUGHED AT
CHRISTOPHER COLUMBUS

THEY ALL LAUGHED AT CHRISTOPHER COLUMBUS

An Incurable
Dreamer
Builds the
First Civilian
Spaceship

ELIZABETH WEIL

Bantam Books

NEW YORK   TORONTO   LONDON   SYDNEY   AUCKLAND

Library of Congress Cataloging-in-Publication Data
Weil, Elizabeth (Elizabeth Ann)
They all laughed at Christopher Columbus : an incurable dreamer builds
the first civilian spaceship / Elizabeth Weil.
p.   cm.
Includes index.
ISBN 0-553-10886-7
1. Hudson, Gary (Gary Charles) 2. Rotary Rocket (Redwood Shores, Calif.)
3. Rocketry—United States—Biography. 4. Space tourism.
5. Outer Space—Civilian use. I. Title.
TL781.85.H83 W45 2002
621.43'56'092—dc21   2002018665

For my parents, Judy and Doug Weil,
and for Dan

The lie of a pipe dream is what gives life to the whole misbegotten mad lot of us. . . .

—EUGENE O'NEILL, *The Iceman Cometh*

THEY ALL LAUGHED AT
CHRISTOPHER COLUMBUS

People have always dreamed of leaving the planet—on the backs of eagles, tied to flocks of trained geese, by magnetic attraction, in a chariot drawn by four red horses in search of Orlando's lost mind, and with the morning dew—and when, in 1969, American astronauts finally reached the moon in a Saturn V rocket, the nature of that dreaming changed for good. The moon voyage offered a trifecta of fulfillment—blasting off on the ride of one's life, tasting the unearthly pleasures of the firmament, and then returning home. It was the dream of adventure, the dream of heaven, the dream of rebirth, all rolled into one. It was, perhaps, the most beautiful dream that ever was, and as such, its apparent attainability confused a generation of American males like few other dreams in our country's history.

Anybody who's ever had a persistent, pressing dream knows that the more one learns about one's fantasy, and the closer one comes to attaining it, the more ornately that fantasy can colonize one's imagination and thoroughly ruin one's life. Just as the address and the work schedule of the beautiful woman can do the crushed-out man more harm than good—providing heretofore unimagined arenas for nuisance and imbecility—so too the details of the coming space age. In 1953, the great missile designer and former Nazi Wernher von Braun—by then living in the

United States—published *Conquest of the Moon,* which included sober, meticulous engineering plans for fifty-seater passenger rockets. Young boys started wearing their mothers' punch bowls like space helmets and walking around in homemade space suits. In 1958, von Braun's fellow German expatriate, the anti-Nazi Willy Ley, followed with *Space Stations,* an honest-to-goodness primer for life on a space colony, where everybody would be smart, the weather would always be perfect, and you could always come in from a space walk, drink a Coke, and radio your girl. Young men began studying naval architecture and preparing careful foam core models of intergalactic ships. So it was not entirely good for mass mental health when finally one day in 1969, there he was: Neil Armstrong standing on the moon, taking snapshots of his buddy, Buzz. NASA had proven it could be done, and like the neighbor who actually wins the lottery or marries the beautiful woman, the feat primarily served to make young earthbound men jealous, and to make Gary Hudson more committed, more attached than ever, to that elusive, tripartite dream.

Gary, then nineteen—sandy-haired, lanky, with a hiccuping, innocent laugh—had grown up in Saint Paul, Minnesota, obsessed with the Disney television series *Man in Space,* and in 1971, he dropped out of college to pursue a career building spaceships with little more to recommend him than an eleventh-grade science fair prize earned from Saint Bernard's High School and a toaster he'd dismantled to look at the parts. Apparently, he'd bought the idea of astronauts as nice boys with short haircuts and pretty wives (not as functionaries in an extravagantly expensive top-priority military game), so he spent the next fifteen years founding and bankrupting rocket engineering companies. He spent two years trying to build a long, skinny rocket called the

Liberty, one year trying to build a "Big Dumb Booster" called the Percheron, and six more working on a short fat torpedo called the Phoenix (for which Tom Clancy helped Gary to raise funds). His only near-success came in 1981: the Percheron reached its launch pad on Matagorda Island, from which it blew up, starting the biggest cow chip fire in Texas history.

Five years later, on January 28, 1986, Gary stumbled downstairs in his Redwood Shores, California, apartment and watched on his television as the space shuttle *Challenger* exploded in a hypergolic burn 46,000 feet above Cape Canaveral, the right solid rocket booster separating from the external tank, the orbiter breaking into several huge chunks, each lighting up in a pure hydrogen-oxygen fireball and each careening downward in a doomed and blazing arc. In NASA parlance, at 12:47 P.M. EST, shuttle mission 51-L "catastrophically disassembled" while traveling at a Mach number of 1.92, killing all seven members of the crew. A horrible tragedy, but for Gary it was oddly tinged with hope. The accident undermined NASA's monopoly in the manned rocket business. With the moon race won and the agency lacking political imperative, chronic space dreamers like Gary now staked a plausible space claim.

At the time of the *Challenger* explosion, Gary's then-company, Pacific American Launch Systems, his fifth thus far, had a contract to build the Phoenix rocket for Society Expeditions, an adventure-trip outfitter selling speculative tickets to prospective space tourists. That he'd proposed the Phoenix at all was an impressive display of self-confidence—the last rocket he'd successfully built and launched was in 1972, from a store-bought Estes kit, a model MK-109 Stingray, sixteen feet tall by one inch wide. But part of the power of a dream is that it whisks the dreamer away from the burden of reason, so after the *Challenger* accident, Gary calmly fielded questions, placating clients who'd called to wonder why, if NASA couldn't build a non-lethal spacecraft, Gary thought he could.

Gary's responses veered toward the philosophic and arcane. His Phoenix, he replied, did not use solid rocket boosters, the shuttle component that first analysis suggested had failed. (Richard Feynman, of course, later set a glass of ice water before the television cameras and proved the culprit to be the O-rings.) Furthermore, Gary submitted, who was to say that NASA itself was good at building rockets? No savvy motorist would buy a government-built car, and no aerospace veteran was surprised when the *Challenger* blew up. As early as 1973, the great von Braun had described the shuttle program as "crossing a river in a rowboat with an elephant in it. When he rocks, you rock. When he doesn't rock, you don't. When you get to the other side, then you think of changing the arrangement."

That morning, along with the *Challenger,* the space race as we knew it—a Cold War duel between two titans—had catastrophically disassembled, but all Gary told his clients was that the elephant had rocked. The next couple of years would be worse than ever for privately-funded rockets, and impossible for sending civilians into space. But after a respectable mourning period— eight to ten years, Gary guessed—the gateway to the heavens would finally open. The *Challenger* debacle had wrested the space fantasy away from the golden boys at NASA. The beautiful bride had left the muscle-bound neighbor, defying social order, exciting disbelief, and though Gary planned to lie low for some time, he knew he'd soon be back, deranged by precedent and addled by desire, chasing that divine and elusive dream. His homespun rocketship hovered just out of reach.

PART
ONE

1

Eleven years later, in the fall of 1997, when Gary told me he'd never been interested in the past or even in the present, that he'd only been interested in the future, I should have been scared but I wasn't, and I should have asked questions but I didn't. I'd just met the chronic and entirely self-taught spacecraft builder for the first time, and I took his statement as a declaration of taste, as if he'd never been interested in money or music, only hot rod cars. Most of what I knew about Gary I'd read in *Halfway to Anywhere,* G. Harry Stine's relentlessly hagiographic 1996 account of the alternative space movement, and I liked to imagine Gary drinking bright volumes of Gatorade at his rocket-building facility in the high California desert, the present filled only with Joshua trees and snakes, the future glaring like the white-hot sun. I imagined myself there, too, swimming in bean-shaped motel pools, living out of my car. Only later, after I'd moved to California and spent three years in Gary's vortex, did I realize what an odd, amnesic place the future is, and that by unmooring himself from past and present, he'd moored himself to nothing at all.

In hindsight, of course, I missed many signals: Gary's near-constant references to *Star Trek* episodes, the near-total lack of successful aerospace experience on the résumés of his employees. But I was more porous than I knew, and that first trip to meet

Gary got off to an auspicious start. I flew into San Francisco and drove south, as directed, on Highway 101, reaching a few miles later the junction of 92, a triumph of light, spirit, and engineering, a place where the ramps angled and arched in such a way that one could imagine driving from the freeway into the sky. Their geometry hinted at weightlessness. Their curves engendered hope. Instantly the ramps convinced me that Gary must pass this interchange every day on his way to work, and that he must more than occasionally wonder if that day, for once, the laws of physics might contain certain loopholes, if Earth might let him go. At least once, I felt sure, Gary must have indulged his curiosity, gunned his roadster up the ramp just to make sure the pavement generated nothing more than some trippy spiritual lift. Of course, he would have found himself not in orbit but on the San Mateo Bridge, on which he would have had to pull a tight U-turn and rejoin 101. From there the directions to his Redwood Shores office would remain the same: exit Ralston Boulevard, right on Twin Dolphin Drive, park in front of Suite 230C, and press through the tinted glass.

I had come to visit because, for a complicated pastiche of political and economic reasons, a small window had finally cracked open on the possibility of civilian space travel, and, from what I'd read, Gary believed unwaveringly, perhaps even unprecedentedly, in the fulfillment such travel provided. He felt the American government had defaulted on the promise of cheap, regular access to space. He was seven when *Sputnik* flew. Nineteen when Neil Armstrong first stepped on the moon. Twenty-two when Eugene Cernan left the last moon-dusted boot mark. And he still seemed not to have fully recovered from the magic of those memories, from the implicit, naïve prospect that someday soon we would all be living in the ether, shouldering power-packs and wearing jumpsuits, in a better, higher, lighter world. Gary's peers included men with Ph.D.s from M.I.T. who had a hard time holding down jobs. One in particular, a man obsessed with the *Star Trek* spin-off *Babylon 5,* remained haunted by a grandmother who shushed him to sleep early on the night of Apollo 17, claiming *you have school tomorrow, you need to be sharp, we'll be landing on the moon every day when you grow up.* (Especially traumatic given that NASA canceled the final three Apollo missions, 18, 19, and 20, the moon shots deemed too expensive, the space race won.) Others gathered annually on July 20, the anniversary of the first moon landing, in Beverly Hills. For their ritual dinner, they borrowed the form of the Passover seder, only instead of commemorating the Jews fleeing the bonds of slavery in ancient Egypt, they celebrated human beings escaping the bonds of gravity here on Earth.

Gary formed his current company, Rotary Rocket, in 1996. For it, he subleased 3,000 square feet of corporate campus space from The Automation Group, a database outfit that soon changed its name to All Bases Covered. At the time, the height of the technology boom, nearly the entire Silicon Valley gleamed— the wet, sodded midways, the kids in their BMWs, the horizon shingled over with futuristic billboards, beating back up into the hills the eucalyptus and Monterey pines. Overhead, just off Twin Dolphin Drive, loomed the six icy mirrored towers of the computer giant Oracle: those fascist-style, triumphant conquering pods, evidence of the seemingly endless money that had washed up on the peninsula in recent years. Rotary Rocket, however, looked outmoded, almost quaint: inside, no security check, no sign-in sheet, just a cozy green velour sofa serving as the waiting area, and airbrushed posters of V-2 and Delta rockets adorning the otherwise plain walls.

That clear fall morning, behind the reception desk, a standard-issue Rand McNally globe wobbled on its stand, and next to the globe sat Anne Hudson, Gary's wife. Anne looked simultaneously vital and sickly, well into her forties, with gentle features, trusting eyes, unfussy hair, an appealing Midwestern directness, twitching hands, and clear plastic braces. Smiling warmly, she pulled the globe off its stand and shifted the sphere from shaking palm to shaking palm. Later, after she replaced it, she tugged open a new pint of cream for coffee and a good quarter-cup spilled on the floor. "It's just been one of those days," she said, setting down her mug so as not to spill it, too. That morning, she confessed, she'd poured a newly-refilled prescription right down the bathroom sink by accident. "Did you see that *Star Trek* episode 'Day of Honor'?" she said, fumbling for the paper towels, cleaning up. "That's where, for one day, everyone on the *Enterprise* finally recognizes all your accomplishments, but for you it just seems like everything's going wrong."

Pictures I'd seen from Gary's early rocket-building days showed a young man, fair and toothy, full of heroic, misguided confidence and steam. Now he poked his head out from behind his office door. At age forty-seven, he still had the same soft mouth, smooth skin, trim carriage, and straight nose, but his eyes were sunk beadily under thick, ridged hoods, his delicate hands shook, like Anne's, and his skull was shrouded in a mat of buzz-cut gray. He'd decorated his office with mementos of his failures, models of his Liberty, Percheron, and Phoenix rockets, and drawings of his Osiris, of which not even models got built. A demoralizing and punitive setting in which to enter one's third decade in the spaceship business, but Gary flatly rejected this theory. "All those past projects were doomed from the start," he said, waving an unsteady hand, his voice an urgent monotone, not unlike Gerald Ford's, "just as the Roton is fated to succeed." Flushed with emotion, he cited the major techno-political and economic changes. "The Cold War has ended! NASA is floundering! Telecommunications giants like Motorola now need thousands of birds launched into space!"

This was all true. The behemoth structures that had supported behemoth aerospace political powers had collapsed. NASA lacked a mandate, the space shuttle never lived up to its sixty-flights-a-year promise, and the public was more reluctant than ever to spend tax money on otherworldly technologies, leaving the space frontier open to fringe capitalistic elements. How, Gary asked, could the U.S. government have ever allowed him to go orbital during satellite spying efforts like Project Corona and the other space-borne espionage schemes of the Cold War? Lacking an answer, I wondered aloud why Gary had continued building his spaceships under such perverse geopolitical conditions. He responded with a question I should have considered more closely: "Why does a fundamentalist pray?"

Gary had grown up an only child in a modest white clapboard house, in what he called "a normal Beaver Cleaver family." His mother, Marcella, was a second-generation Italian housewife; his father, Noble (whose name Gary always coveted), distributed candy and cigarettes to convenience stores and gas stations. The Hudsons never took any family vacations—a fact Gary did not associate with his desire to explore space—and socially he kept to himself, worried even as a child, or so he said, that peer pressure would separate him from his dreams. Gary's formal education consisted of thirteen years of parochial school where he sang baritone in the choir, and while the nuns never managed to shape him into a Christian devotee, they did send him off into the world with a curiously spot-on perspicacity to draw out men's dreams. Once, when I was with him, he pulled into a small-town gas station and said, "What's up?"

The attendant, who had never met him, replied, "Nothing but *Mir*, far as I know."

Gary's desire for space travel took root at age seven, the same year the Soviets launched *Sputnik I,* when he saw an image of a spaceport in *A Trip Through Space,* a cardboard-bound children's primer written by Catherine E. Barry and published in 1954 "for boys and girls ages 8 to 14." Eighty-seven space-related children's books were published in the United States in the 1950s—*You Among the Stars* (1951), *You and Space Neighbors* (1953), *Flash Gordon* (1956), and *You Will Go to the Moon* (1959) among them. But Gary and Anne still referred to *A Trip Through Space* as "the book." They kept a copy of "the book" in a glass-shuttered case in their hardwood-floored living room, above a collection of Anne's most powerful crystals and below a bound volume of Wernher von Braun's engineering plans for passenger buses to the moon. Gary believed that the science fiction he'd read as a child had shaped his sense of what was possible as an adult. Since he'd read "the book," he estimated he'd read about eight thousand others—perhaps a quarter of those science fiction—and drafted a book of his own. He'd seen about a thousand movies, roughly three a month, and even hung the walls of his modern, Mediterranean-style condo with original paintings from science fiction book jackets, but somehow nothing had dislodged "the book" and its spaceport from its pedestal in Gary's mind. On the cover a boy and a girl played with a simple ham radio. One page pictured docks stacked high with boxes for orbital shipping. Another reprinted the space liner schedule: three o'clock departure for Luna, seven o'clock arrival from the asteroid belt.

In his modest office, Gary wore a solid green polo shirt, ironed khakis, Mephisto walking shoes, and a wide leather belt with a large metal buckle in the shape of a Chinese flying fish. "First Lewis and Clark went west. Then the mountain men. Then the trappers and the traders. Then the settlers," he said, positioning his spaceship efforts metaphorically. "What I'm doing here is the mountain man analog." If I understood Gary correctly, he was saying Apollo was Lewis and Clark, the space entrepreneurs (like himself) were trappers and traders, and the settlers would come along very very soon, just as soon as someone developed a cheap, spaceworthy Conestoga wagon—just as soon as his latest rocket, the Roton, took off.

Next Gary lit into a lecture about the various means of capturing the communications satellite market, a market he hoped would lure investment money. "We can lower the price of launch"—of delivering cargo, such as satellites to orbit—"from $5,000 a pound to $1,000 per pound, and at that price we'll still be charging an order of magnitude above our cost." I stared at him, wide-eyed. Eventually, he loosened his shoulders and said, "Look, I don't want to open the space frontier for the goddamn machines!" He took a deep breath and held the air tight inside his lungs. "Excuse my reluctance," he said, exhaling. "It's a vulnerable profession, being a rocket engineer. Being a rocket engineer is actually a lot like being a geeky kid who wants to meet girls. After a certain amount of rejection, what you learn to do is let the girl try to come and meet you."

Rockets originated in China during the Sung dynasty, soon after the discovery of gunpowder, when men learned that if you fill a bamboo with gunpowder and close both ends, you have a bomb, and if you fill a bamboo with gunpowder and close only one end, you have a rocket. The Chinese used their rockets in the defense of Kaifeng in 1232, but the technology was almost entirely forgotten until 1804, when the Englishman William Congreve packed gunpowder into an iron casing and sent it hurtling one and a half miles. Eighty-six years later, Hermann Ganswindt, a German, conceived of the first rocket-propelled spaceship—a major intellectual achievement—but he built nothing, and the idea languished on the outskirts of the theoretical until the self-taught Russian Konstantin Tsiolkovsky published a paper entitled "A Rocket into Cosmic Space" in 1903. Tsiolkovsky later computed gravity-loads, escape velocity, and flight time to the moon, earning himself the moniker "the father of modern rocketry." Still, the first liquid-propelled rocket—the first rocket of the kind capable of escaping Earth's gravity—was not launched until 1926 when a shy and secretive Clark University physics professor named Robert Goddard blasted off a ten-foot-long, magnesium-alloy-and-aluminum airframe, under LOX-ether power, from his Aunt Effie's farm in Auburn, Massachusetts. The rocket soared 41 feet in 2.5 seconds, landing 184 feet away. Only four people witnessed the launch, including Goddard and his wife. No one heard about it for ten years.

Across contemporary culture, space travel has come to mean a great variety of things—the movie *Contact* (1997) represents it as a journey to heaven, the movie *Event Horizon* (1997) as a trip to hell; students once picketed a space art exhibit in Utrecht with posters asking, "Can those who don't believe in God reach heaven by rocket?" To place his own counterculture rocketry in context, Gary offered up a distilled version of space history. "There are two basic ways to leave the planet," he said, "ballistically, atop a missile"—Spam in a can, as the test pilots like to say—"or aeronautically, in a plane." In the 1940s, the United States started looking seriously into both options. On the aeronautic side, the X Program—X for experimental—sought to escape the earth's gravitational field with ever faster and lighter Air Force jets. The first flyer in the series, the X-1, also known as *Glamorous Glennis,* rose to glory when Chuck Yeager climbed in with his dinged-up ribs, breaking the sound barrier in 1947. For the next fourteen years, space planes evolved incrementally over time, up through the X-15, which enjoyed little fame outside the space world, though Joe Walker did pilot it up an unprecedented sixty-seven miles high. But for better or worse—Gary thought worse—in 1961 President Kennedy announced we would put a man on the moon by the end of the decade, and over the few minutes it took Kennedy to deliver his fateful speech, the X program effectively got dropped. Kennedy said, "We go to the moon and do other things not because they are easy but because they are hard," which, to Gary's mind, was really code for saying *we go to the moon not to go to the moon but to prove we can deliver a warhead anywhere we damn well please.* (Tapes recently released by the JFK Library record Kennedy saying in private to then-NASA chief James Webb, "Everything we do [in space] ought to be tied to getting to the moon ahead of the Russians. . . . Except defense, it is the top priority of the United States government. Otherwise, we couldn't be spending this kind of money, because I'm not that interested in space.") But as Kennedy addressed the public, space immediately switched from a place to a national program. Leaving Earth as Spam in a can was clearly the way to go.

In his office, Gary now pulled a red dry-erase marker off the sill of his whiteboard and drew a rough sketch of his Roton—a manned rocket shaped like an upturned egg, with three landing gears at the base and three propeller blades circling the fuselage about two-thirds up.

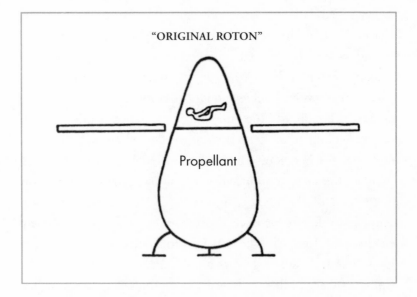

"So this is the original Roton," he said. Above the propellers he drew a stick-figure laid on its back, legs up and bent like an overturned chair. Under the figure, he added a horizontal line and wrote beneath it *propellant*.

Gary hadn't actually come up with the Roton idea himself.

That honor belonged to Bevin McKinney, a long-time rival who, in the spring of 1993, invited Gary to Camarillo, California, for lunch. Only ten days older than Gary, Bevin also had spent almost his entire adult life in entrepreneurial rocket ventures. Like Gary, he too had no formal aerospace engineering training, but he fantasized about opening the galaxy to ordinary men, principally outsiders like himself. At the time of their first meeting, both men had swung from early rocket success clear through to demoralizing failure. In 1981, with funds from a wealthy Houston developer, Gary's simple, liquid-propelled Percheron had become the first private rocket in American history to sit on a launch pad—only to blow up over the Gulf of Mexico. Two years later, Bevin launched his solid-liquid hybrid Dolphin off the coast of Catalina Island. It worked, but his company ARC Technologies soon dissolved for personal and financial reasons.

Bevin's initial idea for the Roton was to use spinning motion—centrifugal force—to hurl propellant into its engines at very high pressures, thereby eliminating the need for the traditional, very expensive, very heavy, and very unreliable turbopumps. Like many good designs, the concept had its own momentum, and Bevin quickly stumbled onto a tantalizing side effect. Spinning motion—in this case, rotor blades powered by small rockets on their tips—could solve one of the biggest problems of any true spaceship: landing back on Earth.

Enamored of the Roton plan, Gary spent the bulk of 1994 working with Bevin to produce various Roton iterations—blades on bottom, blades on top, one conceived in what Gary called "a moment of weakness," which looked like a giant squid—drawing out every possible variant, stalling, or so Gary said, on "bending tin." In early 1995, the two settled on the current design. It was a manned, single-stage-to-orbit, fully reusable rocket—a category of vehicle that had never been built before. For construction, Gary and Bevin intended to do "a Voyager-type thing," meaning, in Gary's particular patois, that they'd build the sixty-five-foot-high rocket-helicopter in a "garage" and then fly it into space.

Alongside the original Roton, Gary now sketched the Roton-C on his board.

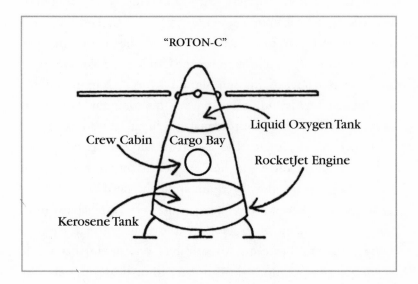

This rocket, too, looked like an upturned egg, only on the skyward end, Gary planned to mount four rocket-tipped rotor blades, each matte black and gangly, just like the blades on a Sikorsky 58 helicopter. On the landward end, Gary intended to install an entirely novel, as-yet-unbuilt, twenty-two-foot-in-diameter rotating engine; called the RocketJet, it would be a

Frisbee-like disk ringed with ninety-six combuster cans, each can slightly larger than a can of Coke. (A combuster can consists of an injector that mixes propellants, a chamber in which those propellants are burned, and a throat-and-nozzle assembly in which the gases resulting from the combustion expand to supersonic speeds.) The interior called for two large tanks, one for liquid oxygen and one for kerosene, a payload bay sized for communications satellites, several football-field lengths of vari-gauged plumbing, and a crew cabin geared for two. If Gary succeeded with the Roton, he would become the first private citizen—the first human outside the Soviet or American government—to build a rocket, put men in it, and hurl them into orbit. Conversely, if Gary failed—if his technology failed—he could be the first man responsible for cutting a ground worker in half with a peroxide-powered tip rocket. Or he would be the first man to send a civilian astronaut to his grave.

In May 1996 Gary wrote a short article on the Roton concept for *Wired* magazine, under the headline "Insane, Or Insanely Great?" He received four or five e-mails from the piece, one from an anonymous investor, and when Gary—then marginally employed, working on an as-yet-unfinished manuscript entitled "Single Stage: The Thirty-Year Quest to Develop Real Spaceships"—bothered to reply, he found that investor to be Walt Anderson. Walt was known in spacer circles as the libertarian, anarchistic chairman of Esprit Telecom, the one and only fund manager of a Tortola-based holding company called Gold & Appel, financial angel behind much of the space counterculture. While Walt fervently insists that his personal worth is only $4 million, through Gold & Appel he had channeled: in 1989,

$80,000 to finance the International Space University; in 1991, $100,000 to found the Space Frontier Foundation; and in 1994, $5,000,000 to start the Foundation for the International Non-Governmental Development of Space (FINDS). Gary, deeply contrarian by nature, responded recklessly to Walt's e-mail—he said he wasn't even sure what he intended to build. Walt, perhaps equally recklessly, responded in a month's time— he told Gary he'd like to invest five million bucks.

Gary projected the cost of developing the Roton at $150 million, not much compared to $6.8 billion for the space shuttle, but still a lot of money. A few weeks after brokering the deal with Walt, he flew to Maryland to visit Tom Clancy's huge, gated estate on Chesapeake Bay. Gary had first met the technothriller writer in 1989, under the auspices of Pacific American Launch Systems, while raising money for his Phoenix rocket. Clancy—an abrupt man with a penchant for flamboyant pronouncements, an irrational fear of airplanes, and little capacity for small talk—had started that first meeting by asking Gary, "How can I help, pal?" Now Gary began, describing the Roton and Walt Anderson. After he finished, Clancy said, "When you close that deal, I know somebody who'd like to invest a million as well."

"Who?"

"Me."

So the Rotary Rocket Company was conceived. Gary incorporated the concern with six other people—Anne; Bevin McKinney; Rick Giarruso, the baby-faced CFO; Tom Brosz, Gary's best friend; Jim Grote, a veteran employee of Gary's; and Dan DeLong, a space fanatic who first met Gary in 1984 and who explained his loyalty by saying, "I believed in Gary and I be-

pounds of thrust when forged. "Everybody else is using surplus Russian engines, which means they're working with existing suppliers that are part of the whole aerospace mafia. But how much are those engines, really? How much will the second one cost? How much will they cost in a year?" His features tightened, as if he suspected conspiracy. "I wanted to call this company Revolution Rocket because the engine revolves and the rotors revolve and it's taking a revolutionary approach to getting into space." He folded up his engine drawing, smoothed its creases against the table. "But our CFO thought that might make the financial community uncomfortable, so we settled on calling it Rotary Rocket."

Next, Gary closed the conference room door and wheeled out the TV and VCR. He cued up a tape entitled REVOLUTION TO ORBIT, and the swirling Rotary Rocket logo—a green sphere wrapped in a red spiral, very cleanly designed—popped up on the screen. A polished British female voice announced, "The way spacecraft are designed in the coming years will change dramatically," and then a white animated Roton rolled out of a gaping hangar, two men climbed aboard, space traffic controllers crackled a few remarks, and the Roton's engines whirled, spewed fire, and the rocket barreled up. Once in orbit, the music of Enya (or an Enya-like substitute; Gary claimed he couldn't afford the Enya rights) faded in and the Roton opened its nose hatch and floated out its payload, and for a brief weightless moment, the world beyond gravity felt narcotic, utopic, impossible to leave. Soon, however—such bliss, it felt too soon—the Roton righted its airframe and unfolded its rotors, enduring the Hadean red heat of descent. Near Earth, the blades pitched down to level and commenced to spin on their own power. The Roton floated and swayed like a leaf. Finally, the spacecraft touched down and the men stepped back onto the ground. The music spiraled to a heady crescendo, and then everything went dark.

Gary sat still a few long minutes. I felt surprisingly moved.

"Pretty inspiring," I ventured, breaking the silence.

Gary replaced the video in its plastic case and slid it across the table. "I guess other people think so," he said, dismissive. "To me it's just another animation. I'm looking forward to the real thing."

2

Six months later, in March 1998, Gary stood slump-shouldered in the parking lot of his Redwood Shores office, the sprinklers ticking in the blue-lawned meridians, the sunlight glinting off the mirrored Oracle buildings and off Gary's new silver, four-door BMW 540i. He had agreed to drive me down to his rocket-building facility in the desert town of Mojave, and as I pulled into the parking lot, he held up a finger, ducked inside his office, and returned with a copy of his Roton video. His hands trembled in the cool air as he motioned me inside his new car's pearly, seal-toned leather. He threw a small purple travel duffel in the back seat. "O let this cup pass from me," he mumbled, and released the emergency brake.

Driving south, listening to Puccini's *Turandot (Vincero! Vincero! Vincero!)*, rolling by the pale green half-cylindrical hangars of the nearby NASA Ames, Gary's hands continued to shake, triggering the wipers and skipping audio tracks—"muscle memory," miscued physical habits from his old Ford Probe, or so he claimed. South of San Jose, the landscape turned from mechanized to pastoral—bright young grasses, Holsteins under craggy live oaks—and in stenchy Gilroy, the garlic capital of the world, Gary pulled over at a gas station and consumed for breakfast one package of crispy M&M's and one package of Donut Gems, and then turned to me and said, straight-faced, "I'm really a Merlot, walnuts, and Brie man." Tangerine oxalis flowered, clover-like, among the early spring garlic shoots. Back in the car, we rose through the cattle-terraced hillsides and over Pacheco Pass. Dirt roads drifted quietly into steep narrow gullies, old horses slept in the shade.

Gary had a habit of self-mythologizing, of saying unbelievable, unexpected things. Chief among them was that he had no interest in building a spaceship. All he'd ever wanted to do, he insisted, was travel in space. "I'm thinking I'll retire when I turn fifty, April 2000," he said, speeding down a relentlessly boring stretch of Interstate 5. "Too much longer, I might not survive. It's a fairly serious burden on your health and your psyche." Trucks whizzed past carrying Ping-Pong balls, Mary Kay cosmetics, and anhydrous liquefied ammonia. "It's kind of like being a quarterback. Do you walk away after the Super Bowl, or do you join another team and play a few bad years and risk breaking your collarbone? I'd rather amass a few credit cards, some cash, and kick back and enjoy the fruits of my labor, and"—this was before his latest comeback—"retire at my peak like Michael Jordan."

Langston Hughes once famously cataloged the things that tend to happen to dreams deferred: they dry up like raisins, or fester like sores, or sag like loads, or explode. Gary's dream had done all these things at different times. In his thirty years in the spaceship business, he'd established and ground into the earth six different rocket companies, and at various times those companies had been broke, flush, and under surveillance by the Soviet government (Gary had painted his Percheron to look as missile-like as possible, and then placed it in full satellite view outside a Lockheed Martin fabrication plant); they had employed six people; employed eighty people; been featured on *Nightline;* shouldered accusations of fraud (had Gary taken investors' money for services he never could have rendered?); and, particularly at Rotary, fought internally like rabid geese.

At present, Gary's dream not only had funding and an outward expression but also competition. Most notably, that competition came from two men named Michael Kelly and Robert Zubrin, and though Gary seemed unfazed by his opponents—at times he insisted he didn't want to be the first into orbit—his corivals gave him context. Early on in my travels in the space world, I went to hear Zubrin address the crowd at Planetfest, a four-day extraterrestrial extravaganza held every year in Pasadena, California. In 1997 it convened over July 4, just as NASA's unmanned *Sojourner* rover was rolling off its lander and onto Mars.

Zubrin had packed the room with space hobbyists, science fiction fans, and awkward, bespectacled boys, various characters who believed they might feel more comfortable off this lousy Earth. "So I am going to talk about how we can send people to Mars," Zubrin started out, "but first I will spend a few minutes talking about how humans have explored the earth." He wore a navy blazer and a too-short tie, and on the overhead, he flashed a slide of the *Gjoa,* a modest, six-person, single-masted boat. "This is a picture of one of the great ships in the history of human exploration of the earth. It doesn't look like a great ship—she's small and not that costly—but it's the ship Captain Roald Amundsen used to make the first successful Northwest Passage." Zubrin explained that before the *Gjoa,* over a hundred doomed attempts had been made—all of them expeditions at least ten times larger. Most notoriously, Sir John Franklin set out in 1854 with two steamer frigates, 127 men, and 300 tons of salt pork. They got frozen in and died to the man, some attempting until the end to salvage crates of fine Victorian china.

"Now," Zubrin continued, small projectiles of spit flying from his mouth, "Amundsen got frozen in the very same place as Franklin and for a longer period of time, but he did not starve. Because Amundsen didn't go into the Arctic with Victorian china and heavy crystal and dress uniforms with shiny buttons. He went into the Arctic with half a dozen hunting rifles and several cases of ammunition plus dogs and men who knew how to use them. The dogs gave Amundsen the mobility to hunt caribou, and that enabled him to live off the land. So the moral of the story is that if you look at the history of human exploration, it has been shown, in fact repeatedly, that a small group of people operating on a shoestring budget can succeed brilliantly when numerous others with vastly greater resources have repeatedly failed."

Part of the frontier mystique is the ability to be scrappy, to make do. One legendary twelve-year-old boy, left to die by his uncle and father near Donner Pass, kept himself alive for an entire snowbound winter by trapping so many foxes he never had to touch the coyote he smoked, roasted, salted, boiled—anything to make it palatable. Rooted in the same self-reliant tradition, Zubrin's Mars plan, called "Mars Direct"—the basis of the science fiction blockbuster *Mission to Mars*—gained its allure from its use of in situ propellant production. This procedure would enable humans to take advantage of Martian natural resources and thus cut the projected cost of a manned Mars mission by a factor of twenty, down to a mere $20 billion.

Mars Direct would begin with an unmanned Earth Return Vehicle filled with six tons of liquid hydrogen that would be jetti-soned on the red planet two years before any humans would go. "So the Earth Return Vehicle lands on Mars," Zubrin said, "and what happens? It goes hunting for Martian caribou, otherwise known as carbon dioxide molecules." The six tons of transported hydrogen would react with the carbon dioxide in the Martian atmosphere, producing 108 tons of methane and oxygen, at a weight savings of 102 tons, a leverage of eighteen to one. "Basically, ours is the Amundsen approach. It's like being able to buy gasoline for seven cents a gallon. Or reaping the useful mass of all the caribou you can eat for the transported mass of several bolts and cartridges."

The aerospace equivalent of leverage or individualism is taking off light. Zubrin hinged his rocket, the Pioneer Pathfinder, on this idea. A somewhat conventional aircraft, the Pathfinder would depart from a coastal runway and then rendezvous with a military air refueling tanker before arching up into the heavens. Like Gary's Roton, it presented a gloriously routinized vision of space travel—around the world in an hour, to space and back in a day. But, primarily because it failed to rival Gary's Roton in the crucial realm of fantasy, and hence the related and imperative realm of fundraising, the Pathfinder would never be built. The false start of aerial refueling failed to grab the imagination the way the Roton did. Nonetheless, Zubrin turned up in Saint Louis in the fall of 1997 for a gala celebrating the X Prize, a $10 million award for the first person or team to fly a vehicle carrying three civilians into space (officially designated as an altitude of sixty-two miles) twice within fourteen days.

The evening felt like a cross between a technology expo with a wet bar and a soap box derby, with the X Prize's fourteen boyish contestants each manning a booth. John Akkerman, the tall, bearded president of Advent International, handed out pamphlets that read YES! NOW YOU CAN TRAVEL INTO SPACE, recruiting members for his Christian space corps. Len Cormier, a red-faced man in his seventies whose wife divorced him over rockets, hawked sweepstakes tickets for his Millennium Express spaceship. Mike Kelly loosened his tie, rheumy-eyed and spent, having mortgaged his house to finance the initial development of his own effort, the Astroliner. The Astroliner was a spacecraft nearly as conventional as Zubrin's Pathfinder, a glider to be towed behind a Boeing 747 until the pilot cut the rope, fired the Soviet RD-120 engines, and careered a hundred miles high.

Gary was not a contestant—Walt Anderson forced him to recuse himself from competition due to bad blood with Peter Diamandis, the X Prize's founder—so the entrant who seemed to have lost the most on his space dream was not Gary but John Bloomer. "This," Bloomer said, waving around a four-fingered hand (he'd blown off a digit as a boy), "literally, is the future of humanity if we have a future." His rocket looked remarkably like a flying saucer. "Our system offers a technology for total and utter conquest both of space and of most of the practical, physical problems of humankind as well." Bloomer wore a forties-style suit and a wide red tie, and he spoke for ten or fifteen minutes without pause. He said he knew how to use laser energy to dart back and forth from Jupiter in just three days, and how to generate atmospheres of breathable air and oceans of drinkable water on Mars. He closed his mouth and crinkled his brow. "Can I tell you something?" he leaned in and whispered. "I've always been five years ahead of my time. It's actually something of a curse."

Much to everyone's chagrin, Burt Rutan, the odds-on favorite for the prize, had stayed home in Mojave, California. Arguably the most innovative aircraft builder in the world, Burt pioneered the use of composite materials in airplanes and conceived and built the Voyager, the first to plane around the world on a single tank of fuel. As a kid he designed new airplanes from the model fliers his brother crashed. As a teen, he won so many model airplane competitions that the associations changed the rules. By middle age, he'd had a heart attack and five marriages. (His first wife left him because, Burt once told a reporter, "there was no question in my mind which I wanted to keep"—her or his first home-built plane.) His achievements now included the Ares, the Pegasus, the Pond Racer, and the Boomerang. Bill Lear consulted plans of Burt's before building his first all-composite jet. Tall, with a nose that swerved to the left, Burt had laconic eyes, muttonchops, and the crazed inward smile of a young Jack Nicholson. For the X Prize gala, he'd submitted a short video statement. "I fully intend to win this thing," he said, caustic, padding in his Birkenstocks around his massive Mojave hangar. "But why would I want to show the competition how I'm going to do it?"

In the humid Mississippi River air, representatives from Space Adventures and Zegrahm Space Voyages—two space tourism companies offering zero-gravity airplane rides and flights in MIG 25s to the edge of space—mingled about, keeping tabs on potential vehicles and hoping to make sales. After the buffet dinner, the night filled with the sounds of Ella Fitzgerald singing the Gershwin standard: *They all laughed at Christopher Columbus when he said the world was round/They all laughed when Edison recorded sound . . .*" and Peter Diamandis, the stocky Harvard-trained X Prize founder, took the podium. "Seventy, eighty years ago," he said, "there were literally hundreds of aviation prizes—prizes for crossing the English Channel, the Atlantic, the Pacific, the United States—and that created the $250-billion airline industry we have today. What we're doing here tonight is predicting the future by creating the future. We're creating a multi-hundred-million-dollar, billion-dollar space tourism industry. We're creating a fast-package and personnel delivery service that will get you or your parcel to Tokyo yesterday, if you're traveling westward. We're talking about the impossible. We're talking about industry. We're talking about doing things in this lifetime that most people never dreamed they'd be able to do."

Throughout the formalities Tom Clancy loitered near the front of the tent, masked in his trademark baseball cap and aviator glasses, chain-smoking cigarettes. Ten seconds before his own keynote speech, he flicked his butt in the grass. "I'm going to start with a quote from George Bernard Shaw," he began, back turned, not quite yet at the mike. "He's a Brit. Maybe you've heard of him? Shaw wrote, 'The reasonable man tries to adapt himself to reality. The unreasonable man tries to adapt reality to himself. Progress, therefore, depends on unreasonable men.' How many people here want to be unreasonable?"

A few hands went up. Everybody laughed nervously. Clancy—six-three and imposing, here with a blonde enormously tall and broad—seemed to enjoy putting people on guard. "Tonight I did an unreasonable thing. I gave $100,000 to the X Prize. I like to put my money where my mouth is—it's a lot of money, it's a big mouth. Share the vision." He went on to spout a kind of cocky patriotism that would come to feel, in the early fall of 2001, hopelessly naïve. "We live in a world today absent the threat of a major war. This is the first time in all recorded human history we have been in this shape. There is not going to be a major war anymore. We fixed it. We have brought peace to the world, we have brought democracy to the world, and now, by God, we're going to bring it to the world out there. This is who we are and that is what we do as Americans."

Running through the history of westward expansion, Clancy noted that governments worldwide, including the United States, were really only good for killing people and breaking things. "NASA," he said, "Not A Serious Agency, is a government-funded airline with 17,000 employees and four planes. We've got to do better. The personal computer was not invented by the government. It wasn't invented by IBM. It was invented by two dropouts named Jobs and Wozniak who started Apple Computer in their garage. That's why you guys are here. We have airplanes flying over us right now. Those were invented here. The telephone was invented here. The telegraph was invented here. We make things new. Our next legacy will be to start human expansion into the future, into the next dimension. Why? Because we're Americans. We do impossible things. Bringing peace to the world was pretty impossible, but we did it. Putting Armstrong and Aldrin on the moon was impossible, but we did it. Possibilities are what we choose to make them. The future is something we will build. That's our job. We're Americans. Thank you very much. Good night."

Gary pulled off the highway midway to Mojave, several miles past the only tourist attraction on the drive—the Harris Ranch, a sort of theme park of the cattle business, with a massive feed lot and a pillar-fronted steak house. For hours, we'd been shadowing the California aqueduct, racing by the patchwork plots, the signs for state prisons and Mercy Springs Road. Ravens flew along fence lines, dry arroyos snaked through fields. At Taco Bell we ate alongside five sullen, crop-weary boys, and after we'd finished, Gary produced a mini Ziploc bag full of vitamins, placed clusters of two or three at a time on his tongue, and chased them down with Coke. He then straightened his neck and stretched his spine. "There's something I think I should tell you," he said. "Since I've been nineteen I've had *two* goals: to journey to the stars, and to live forever."

Two goals! Already the ride had proven to be a kind of tour of the possible: the possibility of squeezing money out of ether, the possibility of growing beautiful produce in the desert, the possibility of sinking a rig down into the soil and drawing oil out of the ground. Now, back on the highway, Gary explained that if the human body did not senesce, the average human lifespan would still only be eight hundred years because people would still die in accidents. He and Anne, he said, regularly attended Anti-Aging Association, or "triple-A," conventions. He knew the difference between nanotechnology and cryotechnology (repairing the body on a cellular level, and freezing the body for future defrosting), between uploading and suspended animation (transferring brain contents to a different body, in which life can continue, and suspending the body before it dies, thereby eliminating some potential problems with revivification). Personally, I'd grown up knowing two great-grandmothers, plus a great-great-aunt Sophie, all bored into crocheting potholders by the time they reached their nineties, Sophie still consuming eggs, bacon, and Bloody Marys and flirting with my boyfriends ("You have a very nice figure," she told one) well past her hundredth year. I had no desire to live eight centuries, and I asked Gary why he did. He made no mention of space travel itself.

"Building a spaceship," he said, "just might take me that long."

At Buttonwillow we headed east toward Bakersfield, into the King Valley, weaving through the almond and pistachio trees buffeted by the wind. Rusted-out farm tools and ramshackle trailers (most likely crystal-meth labs, this being the production capital of the country) dotted the two-lane road. Counterweights of oil derricks swung lewdly in the haze. Once we'd climbed into the foothills the oppression began to lift, the slopes studded with giant boulders called glacial erratics, the valley oaks with their capillary branches almost bare. Cresting at Tehachapi Pass, the road descended into the desert, the greens giving way to browns, the oaks to sage. We followed the wind through an open sand quarry and some violent windmill blades. Then the highway sloped down onto a busted, sand-strewn straightaway, less the crossroads of Los Angeles, Las Vegas, and Reno (as it appeared on the map) than the primary junction of California's central hallu-cinations: the belief that in the future the world will be better, and that in all this austere beauty we will find a way not to die.

Like shards of glass, the abandoned planes popped out of the desert before you could see the few houses in town. The light dominated, artificial and flawless, like a movie set. The power in the electric lines, produced by the nearby windmills at great monetary loss, sounded exactly like a flowing stream. Gary warned me, come summertime, that if I left my Air Nikes in the trunk they might blow up. Nearly two years later I attended a potluck at one of his contractors' homes. The men drank beers on the porch and the women stood cross-armed in the kitchen, as if they were hugging themselves. Mojave surfaced as a topic of conversation. Our host's wife, an open-faced redhead named Ginger, said, "When I got to town I cried a straight week. Mojave makes women cry."

The town had a searching and often tragic history. Honoré de Balzac wrote, "In the desert, there is all—and yet nothing," and the town proved him correct. Founded by the Southern Pacific Railroad in 1876, Mojave first served as a mining outpost—the endpoint for the twenty-mule wagon teams that brought borax out of Death Valley—and later became an aviation center, when the Army Air Corps set up a bombing range nearby in 1933. Since then Mojave had honed its identity, not only from military to civilian flying but as a mecca for emotionally vulnerable fringe technologists. In the early 1970s, for example, Mojave began sponsoring air shows headlined by the Human Fly. An anonymous daredevil who'd lost his entire family in a car crash, or so the myth went, the Fly had been told he'd never walk again. He responded valiantly, if absurdly, by testing "the outer limits of physical and mental endurance," riding bareback atop a DC-8.

Following in the Fly's legacy, a decade later, on July 2, 1982, a Los Angeles man named Larry Walters settled into a Sears lawn chair to which he'd attached forty-two helium-filled weather balloons, intending to fly over the San Gabriel Mountains into Mojave. To regulate altitude, he carried with him an air pistol for shooting the balloons—an ingenious plan, albeit poorly enacted, given that three miles up, Walters's chair tipped slightly and the gun fell to the ground. He then coasted skyward to an alarming 16,500 feet, at which point he was spotted by a pilot who radioed the air traffic control, "This is TWA 231, level at 16,000 feet. We have a man in a chair attached to balloons in our ten-o'clock position, range five miles." Eventually Walters's balloons began to lose helium and after a big, steady drop, he sank into some telephone wires above a former pilot's house. Years later, Walters told George Plimpton, "Life seems a little empty because I always had this thing to look forward to—to strive for and dream about, you know. It got me through the Army and Vietnam—just dreaming about it, you know, 'One of these days . . .'" In the absence of that dream, Walters later shot himself in the heart, only fifty miles from Mojave, while hiking on Mount Wilson.

As viewed from Gary's BMW, the official sign on the outskirts of town read WELCOME TO MOJAVE, HOME OF THE VOYAGER, POPULATION 3,763. Highway 57, on which we approached, split the desert. To its west ran the railroad tracks and the abandoned Casa de Gasa service station; to its east, the dull, venal array of motels and fast food franchises. A mood of depressed violence permeated the town. Behind the franchises festered a ten-square-block scab of dilapidated housing, where kids played war games in small dirt yards and chicken-wire fences held back blowing trash. One did not perceive in Mojave a plethora of options. In fact, within moments of arriving, one felt desperately trapped. Three churches—the Mojave Community Church, the Mojave Church of the Nazarene, and Iglesia Apostolica Central de la Fe en Christo Jesus—all shared a single stucco building. North and south, the roads tapered off or dead-ended in the highway. West they hit the curious horror of the airplane graveyard, 747s tilting nose-first into the sand, flayed Airbuses with picked-over fuselages, the engines, like the eyes of carrion, plucked out first.

"It's clean enough," Gary announced as we passed a neon red

arrow flashing VACANCY for White's Motel. The garbage in the wide street gutters formed suggestive collages: a lilac plastic diaper cover and a fifth of vodka, a bouquet of dirty white carnations and a tab from the Hotel Luxor. Up Belshaw Road, Gary cruised by the boarded-up one-room Kern County Mojave Branch Library and a charred lot where three teenagers banged water barrels like bongo drums. Gary failed to notice the dreariness, or at least to care. He threaded us through a stand of pink-bloomed oleander bushes. "You've just entered the country's first spaceport," he said. Ahead on the pavement stood two gate guards: a cerulean blue Catalina flying boat and a turretless armored personnel carrier christened *The Lady Di*.

Risky aerospace happens where humans refuse to live, and officially we had just entered the Mojave Civilian Flight Test Center, the town's singular claim to fame. The airport, as the locals called it, imposed a three-thousand-acre tract of hangars and air strips atop the aridness. Constructed in 1935 and used during WWII to train Navy and Marine combat pilots, the land was purchased from Kern County in 1971 and turned into a flight test center—logical, given the surrounding population density, lower than around Cape Kennedy or Vandenberg Air Force Base. At the Mojave airport, Burt Rutan had built his Voyager; William Hetrick was accused of running John DeLorean's alleged cocaine cartel (DeLorean was subsequently acquitted of all charges); Kevin Costner had constructed, and subsequently torched, the postapocalyptic tanker in *Waterworld;* and Link Henderson, a luckless local farmer, had dried out a crop of raisins on the runway, spreading seven hundred tons of Thompson seedless grapes.

In early 1997, Gary had informed the airport director, a retired Bakersfield grape farmer, that he wanted to build three Rotons—three because he knew he'd "screw at least one into the ground." Toward that goal, he hired a considerable crew: machinists, engineers, a graphic designer, secretaries, model-rocket hobbyists, a former NASA astronaut who'd never been launched, plus the small band of men who'd worked for him through his previous failures. Also, to fly the Roton, among other tasks, Gary signed on two former Navy test pilots, Marti Sarigul-Klijn and Brian Binnie, each of whom had twenty years military experience, a wife and three children, and, thanks to Gary, a million-dollar insurance policy on his life. Marti—who was shocked to learn from NPR that 99 percent of Americans do not know calculus; how could they get through their days?—had flown over seventy different aircraft and considered himself a practical man: practical in the sense that he researched statistics on highway accidents and decided that he and his family should never again go out on Friday or Saturday nights. Brian—compact and trim, with side-parted brown hair, a Roman nose, and steady eyes—home-schooled his kids, brought a brown-bag lunch to work, and had flown forty-three combat missions in the F/A-18 Hornet off the carrier USS *Midway* during the Gulf War. Those missions included strikes, combat patrols, defense suppression, and utter annihilation of strategic zones, which he referred to as "killbox recce."

The airport spilled across a low ring of buttes backed by mountains with soft folds like crumpled bedding. Gary drove through the blue and white numbered hangars, between which lay a smorgasbord of airplane parts—flaps, wings, tires, landing gear. "That's a Beechcraft Duchess! That's a C130!" he called out, voice raised only slightly above his usual soft patter, wheeling down the tarmac past the vacuum-sealed engine containers and tin-roofed shacks. Vats of Grade A jet fuel squatted behind cyclone fences. Oversize paper drink cups blew across the road. Three men in greasy blue jumpsuits buried their limbs in an aerial refueling tanker that looked like a whale. Gary had driven five hours, 335 miles. He pointed, giddy, hand aflutter, "That's an F4 Phantom! That's an F86! That's a King Air!"

The bright sun made Gary's face look malleable, almost boneless. We wove through a line of wide-bodied planes parked for deep storage and apropos of what—the light? the carnage?—he began telling me that among his greatest regrets in life was not buying a 1949 Chesley Bonestell painting entitled *Zero Hours Minus Five*. I'd seen a reproduction: a romantic, modest, almost airbrushed vision of men in the desert preparing a ship for the moon, the rocket sleek and white and not too huge, the scene bathed in a warm blue light. "I had a chance to buy it in 1989 for $9,500, a really good deal," Gary said, sipping at a bottle of Evian, "it's worth a fortune today. But I had to decline—I was broke from building rockets." He exited the airport's back gate, the gravel rattling his new chassis. "That painting really captures the way things should have been." He quoted Proverbs 29:18: *Where there is no vision, the people perish.* "To have that painting in my possession today, I wish I'd mortgaged my soul."

The thistle, aster, and brittlebrush should have all been in bloom, but scanning the desert I saw only disemboweled remains of L1011s, and a bit of color emanating from a man in a crisp red-and-white plaid shirt who was wandering among the sparse desert holly and salt bush, herding a flock of sheep. He rocked his head back in a greeting; Gary raised a hand. Neither of us commented on the impossible strangeness. In fact, neither of us said anything until Gary reached a bend in the road marked by a pile of discarded missile parts, their once-glossy coats faded to a delicate robin's-egg blue. Here he idled the motor and stared into the cracked hardpack, his brow, straight nose, and pink-bowed mouth all in a stacked line. Several ewes slept in the shade of a wheel-less jumbo jet. Gary pressed a finger up to the windshield glass. "Right out there," he said, "is where we're going to build our launch pad."

The empty desert stretched for miles to the mountains—just sage, more sage, and Joshua trees, and a dirt trail worn to a polish by jackrabbit and coyote feet.

3

In *The American West as Living Space,* Wallace Stegner writes of pioneers hitting the ninety-eighth meridian, the edge of the desert, as reaching "the border of strangeness." "Almost all the new animals they saw," he writes, "they misnamed. The prairie dog is not a dog, the horned toad is not a toad, the jackrabbit is not a rabbit, the buffalo is not a buffalo, and the pronghorned antelope is more a goat than an antelope." Such lapses say something not only about the exotic local fauna but the people who are drawn to the West—not men with taste for roots and patience for linguistic history, but *pueri aeterna,* eternal boys, Adams before the fall, recklessly naming the world as they see it, even if they are wrong.

In her book *Puer Aeternus,* the Jungian psychologist Marie-Louise von Franz describes the puer condition—arguably a prerequisite for any man drawn to the frontier, certainly a prime component of Gary's psyche—as charm mixed with a provincial late-adolescent arrogance, merged inferiority and messianic complexes, asocial individualism, fear of being pinned down, a powerful craving for heights (often resulting in airplane and mountaineering deaths), and a refusal to adapt to the mainstream world because that world obscures his hidden genius. Gary's hero, Antoine de Saint-Exupéry—the aviator, engineer, and author of *The Little Prince;* according to von Franz, the consummate puer—disappeared in his plane over the Mediterranean. "Oh! I have slipped the surly bonds of Earth/. . . and done a hundred things/You have not dreamed of . . . ," writes John Magee in his poem "High Flight." His sentiment fuses the space traveler fantasy and the most basic puer desire.

When in Mojave, I slept at the all-too-earthly White's Motel. The place was owned by Roger White, then eighty-three years old, and it had been in the White family since 1905, when Roger's uncle, George, trekked out to work on the railroad for reasons that over ninety-four years had boiled down to "Mississippi was rougher than heck." My first night involved what I believed to be my first earthquake but turned out to be a passing train. The following morning Gary escorted me to Mojave Civilian Flight Test Center Building 31B, the façade of which looked like an oversize, steel-corrugated shoebox squatting in a gravel parking lot strewn with dismantled planes. Inside, the space felt exciting, unfinished, like a sky preparing to rain. Telephone cords and power lines vined down from the ceiling. Pale-skinned men strode from copy machine to bookcase, arguing about terms like "transonic trajectories," and "angles of attack." Office trailers propped up on stilts lined the east end of the building. Between them lay a swatch of tight flat carpet, and on the carpet sat clustered a dozen mismatched desks.

At one of these desks, Brent Eubanks—an enormous twenty-six-year-old, as awkward as a walrus—studied the physics of stoichiometry (the art of mixing oxidizers and fuels), his straggly blond hair pulled behind his head in a ponytail, a small leather pouch tied around his neck. By way of introduction, Brent told me that he knew how to fix every piece of machinery in use in his daily life—his computer, his oven, his car, his VCR—but he couldn't parse a line of poetry. "Poetry is analog," he said, his voice leaning into his words. He borrowed a sheet of notebook paper. On the paper he drew a curve, and under the curve he traced a series of lines, the tops of which shadowed the arc.

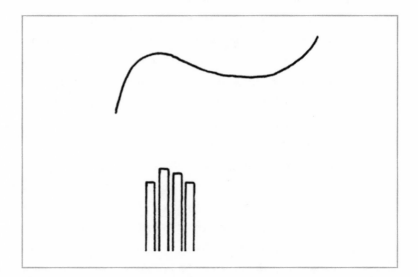

"The curve is analog," Brent said, handing me back the notepad. "I only understand digital. The lines are digital."

Brent had moved from Boulder, Colorado, only two months earlier. He described Mojave as "hard on humans, not hard on machines," and he'd come to California "to help build a rocket, because that's just so cool." Here the state motto remained *Eureka!* I've found it! Here hope met destiny, and new arrivals forcibly assured themselves that things would work out, because this was where they ran out of continent. Like the men in the late-nineteenth-century West who'd asked one another, "What was your name back in the United States?" (the implication being they'd all been someone else), Brent sought "freedom from the weight of history, from the stupid rules, from the stupid people." He had been, by his own admission, a social outcast since kinder-garten—"a geek in grammar school, a geek in middle school, a geek in high school, the geekiest guy in the geekiest crowd at Caltech, and probably the geekiest guy here." His parents studied Ayn Rand, raised him as a rational objectivist, and signed him up for karate classes so he could make some friends. At age four he started dreaming of leaving the planet. At age six he read about Gary in a "science fact" magazine.

Now Brent worked on Gary's propulsion team, building the twenty-two-foot-diameter, ninety-six-combuster RocketJet en-gine under the leadership of an electrical engineer named Jeff Greason. (Later, when I asked Jeff what made him want to go to space, he replied, "What made you first want breathing?") Wait-ing for his microwave popcorn to pop, Brent shoved his hands into his pockets and told me about a college friend, an electrical engineer or "double-E," by the name of Paul. "Paul had this weird ability to connect with other people on an emotional level that the rest of us in our group just didn't seem to have. We all came up with a word for this skill—we would call it *telepathy*." Across the hangar, on the bare cement, sprawled Craftsman tool boxes, lathes, drill presses, an impressive assortment of disassem-bled motorized vehicles, a half-dozen coffin-like boxes filled with hay and helicopter rotors, and several oily helicopter transmis-sions dripping over drums. Brent laced his direct speech with incomprehensible jargon. "I mean, what else would you call understanding what's going on in a remote receptacle for the case in which that receptacle does not emit quantifiable data about what's going on?"

To impose discipline on his engineering crew, Gary called a "baseline review meeting" every Friday morning, which he attended religiously, primarily for his own satisfaction, either in person or over the phone. This particular Friday, just before its ten o'clock start, he stood in the gravel parking lot outside Building 31, watching a trio of slate gray F4 Phantoms glide across the sky. The sun had risen quickly, casting a yellow sheen across the pink-and-tan alkali flats. "The Roton is going to be my last and final effort," Gary told me softly, drawing a hand across his forehead to shield his eyes. "I've discussed this with Anne and with most of the company founders, but I'd prefer you keep it quiet from the employees." Not out of deceit or pride or fear, Gary explained, but to protect from unnecessary anxiety his loyal crew, those for whom Gary's rocket ventures had become a way of life.

Entering a conference room a few minutes later, we joined thirteen engineers around a rectangular folding table, most of them sun-weathered and in their forties, but with younger men's eyes. The group consisted of several members each from Gary's engineering subgroups—propulsion, airframe, and rotor—plus representatives of the test site team and from his prime subcontractor, Burt Rutan's Scaled Composites. A fan whirred in the doorway, sucking in air and flies. Impressive, poster-size Roton line drawings flapped from cork strips glued to the walls. Gary pulled loose a plastic chair, cased his sunglasses, and slid on his half-cut reading lenses. His hands spasmed a moment atop the long, plastic tabletop. He then pulled the lenses off his nose, choosing to spin them by the bridge instead.

The meeting felt like a game of playing rocket company, condensed, poignant, and gestural. "Okay," said Marti Sarigul-Klijn, Rotary's chief engineer and lead test pilot, swatting a few bugs from his face, "what we need to do today is down-select some gear." Marti's job at Rotary was to turn the Roton concept into a functional design, deliver that design to Scaled Composites, and then, along with his co–test pilot, Brian Binnie, test the resulting prototype. He stood in front of the overhead projector, a tall man with metal-framed glasses and a mischievous face, dressed in chinos, a plaid shirt, and a bomber jacket, all army green. In his twenty years in the Navy, Marti had flown the Grumman A-6E Intruder (all-weather attack), the Grumman F-14A Tomcat (fleet air defense, air-to-air combat), the Grumman EA-6B Prowler (electronic warfare, radar and radio jamming), the Lockheed S-3A Viking (anti-submarine), and the McDonnell-Douglas FA-18D Hornet (fighter bomber). Now, from his home in Davis, California, he flew to work every morning in a beat-up Yankee Grumman as small as a station wagon. If he flew to the Redwood Shores office, Marti would then Rollerblade to Twin Dolphin Drive, replete with knee pads, elbow pads, helmet, and a rearview mirror—this in addition to his tattered soft-brimmed khaki hat and the orthodontic metal retainer that streaked across his teeth.

Marti's nickname in the Navy had been Data, in tribute to the android on *Star Trek,* and before retiring he spent six weeks interviewing around Lockheed Martin and McDonnell-Douglas. Then he spotted a flyer for a talk at NASA Ames: "Roton Development and Flight Test Program: Single Stage to Orbit," by Gary Hudson. Initially, Marti told himself he'd be attending the lecture for sport—"to see how this Hudson guy would handle what was sure to be a hostile audience"—but by the night of the lecture, which was, as it turned out, the night of his ninth wedding anniversary, he'd studied the Roton concept with such interest and rigor that he'd prepared three pages of single-spaced questions, some of which pointed toward technical issues Gary had not yet even considered. On the spot Marti decided to work for Rotary—what test pilot could resist the chance to become the first civilian astronaut, or at minimum to test an entirely novel helicopter? The choice, however, nonplussed his wife. A professor of aerospace engineering, she'd been hoping to hire her husband herself.

Back in the trailer, Marti projected on the wall behind him a military cartoon caricaturing fifteen different airplanes designed by fifteen specialty groups—the armament group's plane loaded down with weapons, the service group's covered over in hatches, the power plant's plane a bulging engine with propellers and small stubby wings. "I understand everybody has different preferences," Marti said deliberately, straining for a consensus. "The engine team wants the gear to be ultralight. The rotor team wants the gear to be stiff. Of course Brian and I want the gear to be extremely reliable." He cracked his knuckles and broke into his orthodontic grin. "But very deep in our hearts," he said, "I think we can all agree that we want the gear to be lightweight."

This was neither purely an emotional nor an analytical statement. It was a fantasy couched in engineering terms, and as Marti voiced it, chins bobbed around the table, indicating that Marti had passed some test. The nature of that test—a test of one's ability to articulate the dream of space in a realm without the possibility of real success or real failure—was not yet obvious to me. But I knew that with few exceptions, both Marti and Brian among them, most of Gary's senior people had been working for him for a long time. They'd worked for Foundation, Inc., founded by Gary in 1970 to build a single-stage reusable rocket called the Osiris and disbanded in 1979 for lack of funds; for GCH, Inc., founded by Gary in 1980 to build the Percheron and disbanded in 1982 after the Percheron blew up on the launch pad; for Pacific American Launch Systems, founded by Gary in 1982 to build a single-stage reusable rocket called the Phoenix and disbanded in 1989 for lack of funds; and for HMX, Inc., founded by Gary and Bevin McKinney in 1994 and mothballed in 1996 when Rotary Rocket was formed. "I can't imagine working for anybody else!" one veteran explained during a coffee break. "Working for Gary is the greatest job in the world! We were so young when we started out! You should see the pictures!" He stopped, blinked, collected his enthusiasms. "It's like we're one big family! Sometimes a little dysfunctional, maybe. But we're like a group of brothers. We all know each other extremely well. We can all be fully ourselves."

Stegner defined the Western costume as "the boots, spurs, chaps and sombrero bequeathed to him [the archetypal Westerner] by Mexican vaqueros, plus the copper-riveted pants invented for California miners by Levi Strauss." No one here wore any of it but Levi's—Marti never got dressed in the morning without donning at least one article of clothing colored khaki or army green—but all nonetheless filled the legendary Western man's role: "the historical pioneer, the lone-riding folk hero . . . the freedom-loving loner . . . estranged from real time, real place, and any real society or occupation." Gary's best friend Tom Brosz articulated the Western-Rotary connection succinctly. "You ever seen that Clint Eastwood movie *Bronco Billy*?" he asked me one day over turkey and mashed potatoes. "The guy just decides he's a cowboy one day. He starts doing the job, dressing the part. And you know what? He is one."

It provided a certain continuity—the prairie dog is not a dog, the engineer is not an engineer. "I'll tell you one thing," he added, attempting to make sense of a career largely in Gary's employ. "Maybe I could have gotten an engineering job at Lockheed making some part of some widget which attached to the lower left whatever of some high-flying booster, but I don't think that would have been a better life. You know? You can be a technician and set up the stage for bands and tell all your friends and yourself you're in the music business, and in a certain way you wouldn't be wrong. But no matter how well you set up the lights, they're never gonna let you play the drums."

Marti spent the remainder of the meeting flashing slides on the projector like a lens-fitting optometrist. First he individually presented the three main landing gear contenders—folding legs, telescoping legs, legs that popped out into the shape of an A. Then he flashed the choices in pairs, asking *which is better, A or B? Which is better, A or B?* Throughout this most of the guys swatted flies, and did so in a controlled, engineering fashion—with enough force to inflict a mortal wound, but not so much as to produce a disruptive noise. Steamroll a fly under a coffee Thermos. Pinch one, Zen-master style, between two sharpened pencils. Eventually the gallery selected the A-shaped legs, after which Marti ceded the floor to the Roton's original inventor Bevin McKinney, who reported that a few days earlier Scaled Composites had mounted a 15 percent scale model Roton on the front of a pickup and driven it down a Mojave runway, providing "a SWAG as to the Roton's stability and air flow"—a crude wind-tunnel test. And so the meeting ambled along according to its own bizarre vernacular, Gary remaining silent throughout. In the corner, the pilot Brian Binnie, an even straighter arrow than Marti, quietly blackened a leaf of graph paper. That is, until one of Gary's old-timers killed a fly and raised two arms overhead. At which point everyone, including Gary, clapped and left the room.

4

L ater that spring, for an engine test, Gary drove down to Mojave again. His test site occupied a circular tract five miles
past the airport into the desert snarl, where wood rats and black-
speckled lizards scurried across the sand, pausing with confusion
at the double-wide trailers and the cement foundations of Gary's
test stands. In the center of the site stood the blockhouse and the
office trailers; farther out, the tool sheds and the stands themselves. All structures carried four-part, diamond-shaped warning
placards rating health hazard, fire hazard, reactivity hazard, and
material hazard on scales from zero (lowest) to four (highest). In
the center they read in zeros and ones, like computer code, and
on the outskirts, in threes and fours, like key signatures for a
waltz.

For the sake of clarity, it may help to know that a test stand is
exactly what it sounds like: a strong, sturdy platform, plumbed
with fuel lines, on which one mounts a rocket engine, firing
either toward the horizon or straight down. Gary's strongest test
stand, R1, had a horizontal firing threshold of 100,000
pounds—it could secure to the ground an engine emitting that
amount of force—and it sat inside what appeared to be a prefab
gardening shed, the stand itself a table bolted to the foundation,
entwined in yards of ornate pipe. Gary's oldest stand, H1—H for

HMX, Inc., Gary's mothballed company—was tall, red, and propped up on stilts, resembling a beach house rising over the tide. Combined, Gary's stands could withstand 660,000 pounds of thrust, the equivalent of 190 late-model Ford Mustangs gunning at full steam. Thus far the test site had produced only 7,000 pounds of thrust, total—1.4 percent of the half million pounds of thrust animated in the launch in Gary's Roton video.

In addition to the traditional vertical and horizontal rocket test stands Gary had also built a whirl stand, an upright assemblage of rotors in a thirty-five-foot-deep sandy pit, like an umbrella in a rum drink. Gary planned to use the whirl stand to test the tip rockets mounted on the Roton's helicopter blades. (The small rocket engines would cause the propellers to spin. The propellers would be fitted with fuel lines.) At the bottom of the pit lay a large cement disk, thirty-five feet in diameter by two feet deep. Anchored to that disk was a steel-trussed pole. Fitted to the pole, a helicopter transmission. Balanced on that transmission, four rotor blades. And bolted to each blade, a custom-made tip rocket, a peroxide-powered thruster capable, in theory, of lifting the Roton against the force of gravity as Marti or Brian piloted it down to land. Several weeks earlier, during the whirl stand's construction, a leather-skinned man with bowed legs and a cowboy hat had knelt in his kneepads and rolled a stake of rebar between his palms. "This here's my 1965 Chevrolet," he'd said, perhaps to the universe, perhaps to himself. "These guys are gonna make history here." He took a mallet and whacked the rod into place. "It's good to be part of history. Not every man gets to help build a spaceship. I'd like to come out here one day, watch them fly these things one time."

A better understanding of the Roton—particularly its two

main subsystems: its rotor, or landing system, and its engine, or ascent system—may be in order. For landing, Gary planned to use tip-rocket propulsion—the small rockets on the ends of his rotor blades—and this technique was proven, if not mainstream; it had been around since the World War II German *Triebflügel*, or propeller wing, which could take off and land anywhere, fly at nearly Mach 1, and rise in ten minutes from zero to 30,000 feet. Later, in the 1950s, both Americans and Europeans manufactured tip-rocketed helicopters (some were deployed in Vietnam), and in the 1960s, NASA even attached free-spinning rotors to a scale-model Apollo capsule, attaining speeds of Mach 15. But while the Roton's rotor-based landing system was at least loosely proven, its spinning-based ascent system, the RocketJet engine, was not. Nobody had ever hurled fuel to ninety-six combusters ringing a spinning disk. How to do this was not well understood, not least because spinning itself is a far more complicated proposition than it at first might seem.

According to *Physics for the Inquiring Mind,* a ten-pound textbook, when a force pulls toward the center of an orbit it is called a centripetal force, and when a force flies out from the center it is called a centrifugal force. Gary and Bevin designed their rocket around these forces. Specifically, they designed the spinning engine around centrifugal force—with the hope that the force flying out from the center would transport rocket fuel to its outside ring of combusters—the same force at work at the carnival when the bottom drops out of the Tilt-A-Whirl. At the start of that ride, you strap yourself in, back flush against the wall, at which point the room begins to gyrate and the floor falls out. But in trying to assess what's going on, intuition can be misleading. You feel as though your body is being pushed outward, slammed to the wall—you feel the force Gary and Bevin were counting on to transport their fuel—when in reality all that's happening is that your mass is trying to follow Newton's First Law, the law of inertia, and just keep traveling in a straight line in the direction it's been going.

How to deal with the misapprehension? After numerous examples involving square dancing, lassos, and playground equipment, the author of *Physics for the Inquiring Mind* offers several ideas for dealing with our lost bearings, in particular for dealing with that perceived flinging-out-from-the-center force, which does not in fact exist. The first suggestion is to retrace one's logic, to consider a misinterpretation of evidence (I feel as though I am being flung outward but I am not). The second is to look at emotions (to admit, perhaps, that you might be self-deluding, living in a rotating system and trying to forget this). And the third recommendation the author offers only tentatively, and refers to winkingly, as "The Engineer's Headache Cure." He concedes that the feeble-minded, fainthearted engineer might try to ease his brain strain by turning a spinning problem into a static equation (make the problem easier by joining the spinning world). But by doing so, he negates the possibility of learning anything about true nature. He buys a correct response to his homework at the expense of understanding itself.

Gary employed a fourth method: he dealt with the complexities of his spinning engine by putting off the problem. Quite logically, he argued that before he could even begin exploring the spinning mechanism of his ninety-six-combuster RocketJet engine, he first had to build and test a single functioning rocket combuster, one of the eight dozen that would eventually stud the ring. The physics of this, the physics of combusters, rests on a different law of mechanics, Newton's Third Law. That law states that for every action there is an equal and opposite reaction. It explains why a gun kicks back when it shoots, and why, if you fall off a footstool or out of an airplane, the ground hits you as hard as you hit it.

In the case of a rocket engine, Newton's Third Law expresses itself the way an inflated but untied balloon zips around a room. (An inflated but tied balloon stays still because the puffed-in air pushes on all sides equally.) With the untied balloon, the puffed-in air pushes on the inside front wall, urging the balloon forward. In reaction, the front wall pushes back, sending gases streaming out the open rear. Tapping this energy of imbalance, a rocket engine operates like a machine gun mounted on a rowboat, and the technology has existed, in one form or another, since 360 B.C., when the steam-powered Pigeon of Archytas skated across a wire. Rockets are simpler, at least in theory, than combustion engines, steam engines, diesel engines, and turbines. In fact, rocket engines only get complicated when one gets ambitious, taking words like *very* and *rapidly* to their extremes. To move something *very* rapidly forward—that is, to move something else *very* quickly out the rear—one has to pump something *very* cold (like liquid oxygen) into an open cavity and turn it into something *very* hot (like a super-rich flame). In Rotary's previous engine test, the liquid oxygen and kerosene had produced more heat and pressure—6,000 degrees, 300 PSI—than the stainless steel chamber could handle. The engine had burst and melted into a piece of slag.

Today's engine test was a second attempt to find materials and fabrication techniques capable of withstanding that intense pressure and heat. For it, several engineers joined Gary out at the site, exchanging the minimal niceties with the test site workers. But only one of Gary's engineers felt truly comfortable out here: Christopher Smith, a young man who often spent his lunch breaks exploding homemade solid rocket propellant shavings behind Building 31. Twenty-six, lanky and loping, with cowboy good looks and hair the color of burnt grass, Christopher had discovered firecrackers at age seven. Then at fourteen, because his father would buy him firecrackers only on the Fourth of July, he'd discovered model rockets. Now he lived twenty miles from Mojave in the busted development town of California City, in a three-bedroom, ranch-style house he rented for $450 a month, the kitchen counters lined with mason jars containing ginger snaps, M&M's, ammonium perchlorate, chewing gum, strontium sulfate, and rice and pasta, in no particular order. One day, hoping to understand his affinity for pressure and heat, I met him at his house to hike up a scree-covered butte outside of town. The ground powdered and cracked beneath our feet as we walked through a field of abandoned and rusting household appliances—washing machines, refrigerators—which Christopher fantasized about filling with flash powder and watching blow up. "If I ever have a lot of money," he said, "I want to become a philanthropist. I want to sell firecrackers at cost to the poor." On top of the butte we ate barbecued sunflower seeds. "One thing I don't understand about the Bible," he said. "Heaven must be the place that's full of fire. Hell must be something else."

On the test stand that day Gary had placed a 1.2-inch stainless steel LOX-kerosene engine, a stainless steel can with an inner cavity 1.2 inches in diameter into which liquid oxygen and kerosene would flow, expand and, sparked by an igniter, burn. The can was smaller, heavier, and much less powerful than those the RocketJet would eventually require, and shortly after the engineers arrived at the site, one of Gary's old-timers, a round white-haired man, emerged from the blockhouse to deliver a safety lecture. He pointed to a huge white tank (20,000 gallons of water for emergency fire-fighting) and to a red shed gnarled with plumbing (the "live" test stand, scheduled to fire in thirty minutes). Then he said, "This is an official hardhat area," a massive understatement since an explosion could have caused serious injury, perhaps even death. "We maintain pressurized fluids out here at all times. Watch where you put your feet and where you put your hands. Don't lean over hoses with end-fitting on them. Don't act stupidly. Don't bump your head. No smoking allowed at the site."

Afterward, a group of site hands crowded inside one of the brown-carpeted trailers, discussing not the engine test—by and large, the test site workers were Antelope Valley locals and not space obsessives—but who would make the acetylene bombs for the Fourth of July and who would make the flash powder. Most of these men now had, thanks to Gary, something of which they'd never dreamed, a job about which they cared. One, a skateboard punk named Johnny Hernandez, extravagantly pierced and tattooed, stood in front of the open refrigerator gulping apple juice from bottles shaped like grenades. Brown-skinned, twenty-two, moody, with an irrepressible sparkle, he was dressed in long plastic gloves, metal ankle gaiters, and a hard hat decorated with a mohawk of screw protectors, stickers from Alpha Explosives, and a rabbit's foot dangling off the back. For his last job, he'd installed cab-over campers in Palmdale. Now he plumbed lines for engine tests. For the benefit of the young secretary with the tawny legs and beaded anklet, he informed the room that his pit bull had recently killed his girlfriend Faydra's dachshund. Of one of his more thuggish co-workers he asked, "You buy those shorts or you steal 'em?" Then he punched at the trailer's spring-hinged door and pushed into the blazing heat for some last-minute purging of lines outside.

Once the test site crew left, the propulsion team—Brent, Christopher, and the others—just waited, sitting cross-legged on the trailer floor while Gary read *SpaceNews* in a folding metal chair, his forehead drooping toward his knees, his nose pointed toward his lap. At the front of the trailer on a monitor you could see the engine on the test stand looking like a heart in an exposed chest cavity—the shed doors swinging open like cracked ribs, arteries of plumbing entwining a powerful, intricate knot. Audible through the closed-circuit TV link, the test commander, a former Silicon Valley whiz kid currently next door in the blockhouse, ran down his pre-test checks: "Number nine: Check the controls and the igniters under pressure. Number ten: Purge the igniter system with H_2." A white band of frost crept along the liquid oxygen line. When the LOX reached its tank, it instantly broke into a boil: a minus-300-degree liquid in a ninety-eight-degree desert: it sounded like the largest teakettle in the world.

In *Flight into Space* (1954), Jonathan Norton Leonard wrote, "To watch the test of a rocket motor is a shattering experience. The eyes cringe from the light, and a wave of heat beats against the skin. An indescribable bellowing sound pokes like an ice pick into cotton-stuffed ears. Even worse than the bellowing is a high-pitched waspish scream. This is the faintly audible edge of the motor's ultrasonic sound. It tears at the heart and groin and raises knife-edge vibrations echoing inside the skull." Fortunately, by the late 1960s all rocket tests were controlled remotely. So today at Gary's test site no engineers suffered ice picks to the ears or waspish screams. Instead, from the trailer, they listened intently to the countdown, that interminable descent from ten, Gary staring at his magazine until the count of five, his eyes not focused on the screen until the count of one. Half a second later, the igniter popped, the gases hissed, and the engine ejected a retching, if modest, *BOOM*! The blast sounded like a small waterfall, a phenomenon clearly impressive in kind, but limited by its scale. For a moment, the flames gushed out of the rocket's throat, sleek, constrained, and smooth. But then they fractured, odd-angled and in vain. The nozzle puckered and the metal sagged as the engine ripped itself apart.

"God damn it!" Brent and his propulsion chief boss both shouted at once, their voices bouncing around the trailer until Christopher rewound and replayed the tape. This time in slow motion: the surge of fire split into a scatter of flames, and then backward, the scatter re-collected itself into a surge. Christopher replayed the tape again and again, like an old home movie. Backward provided a giddy timeless pleasure, the world as it cannot be, the uncle flying back onto the diving board, the water splashing back into the pool.

Finally, Gary coughed and stood up, delivering an offhand sermon on welded flanges and streamlined geometries, explaining how the low graphite quality had caused the chamber to erode from the nozzle, and how, because of faulty O-ring placement, the seal had frozen and the LOX had "invaded," causing heats and pressures far too high for the stainless steel chamber to hold. In the sinking sun, Johnny the skateboard punk vented the tanks and purged the tubing lines, releasing icy-pure oxygen into the dusty desert air. On a whiteboard, Gary sketched a few quick redesigns for his crew. Then, the field declared clear and safe, Gary motioned his engineers to follow him outside.

The tableau at the test stand felt disastrous and triumphant, like the photograph of Iwo Jima. Gary shone a flashlight into the metal while his men knelt before him in twos and threes, eyeing the mangled crater where there had been a perfect, round core. Fearless, almost paternal, Gary towered as his engineers crouched, gawking at the fruits of their failure, staying on until the yucca moths emerged and the night snakes slipped out. Only later, over dinner at Grazziano's Pizzeria—two booths filled up with engineers, Peter Jennings on the nightly news warning of an asteroid that might hit Earth—did I think to ask Gary why he was not upset.

Confessional, he pulled me aside, turned his back to the crowd. "To be honest," he said, "I knew this engine would fail. I have to train a new generation of rocket engineers, so I let them make mistakes—unless they're grossly expensive, or dangerous, or both."

5

What passes for a "normal" rocket-building process varies greatly, though Jan Roskam's eight-volume *Airplane Design* does spell out one generally accepted approach. Step one is research, planning, and conceptual design, and consists of determining the vehicle requirements—manned? unmanned? 1,000 pounds into orbit? 7,000 pounds into orbit? (For the space shuttle this took a year and a half.) Step two is development or preliminary design, sketching the particulars of the vehicle itself—deciding which technologies make the most sense. (For the space shuttle this took two years.) Step three, detailed design, consists of finalizing the vehicle's specs for prototype production. (For the space shuttle this took three and a half years.) And step four is testing, working out the prototype's bugs for manufacture. (For the space shuttle this took four and a half years.)

Contradictory examples abound—Gary often cited aviation history, in particular the P-80 fighter, built during World War II in only 143 days—and he too hoped to save time and money by working on a compressed schedule. Step one, conceptual design, he'd completed with Bevin McKinney prior to founding the company, and now he intended to elide steps two, three, and four, simultaneously designing and testing the Roton components (such as the combuster can) and commissioning his first prototype.

This prototype Gary called the Roton Atmospheric Test Vehicle, or ATV. It would be a full-scale resin-and-carbon-fiber cone, sixty-five feet high, but with no spinning RocketJet engine—in fact, no engine at the base at all—just an airframe topped by a halo of rotor blades, each fitted with a small tip rocket on its outward end. This vehicle Gary referred to as his "landing gear demonstrator," and in it Marti and Brian, the two pilots, would test the feasibility of the rotor, or landing, system. To do this, the pilots would put the ATV through a series of incremental flight tests: first a ground test, then a hover test, then a down-the-runway flight, and finally an up-and-over mission, during which Marti and Brian would fly the ATV up to 2,000 feet, kill the power to the tip rockets, and see if they could still land.

After Gary built the ATV—or rather, after Scaled Composites built the ATV; Gary had subcontracted it out to them—he intended to build the PTV-1 (the Propulsion Test Vehicle-1), which, under the power of an ordinary rocket engine, would fly up to 500,000 feet and deploy the main rotor system; the PTV-2, which would fly suborbital and orbital profiles under power of a RocketJet engine; and then production-model Rotons. Toward that goal, early on in the Roton project, in an official publication wishfully titled the RAPID (Rotor and Airframe Program, Interim Development), later retitled the R2D2 (Rotary Rocket Design Document), Gary issued this engineering bull:

Group:

Bevin and I have set weight targets for vehicle subsystems. Some of these are more challenging than you might have wished, but we'd like to aim low and push the technology a bit. Let's see what can be done.

Airframe	4,000 lbs.
Rotor	2,500 lbs.
Crew cabin	600 lbs.
Gear	1,000 lbs.
Avionics and power	500 lbs.
Pressurization (empty)	500 lbs.
RCS/OMS (empty)	500 lbs.
Main propulsion (dry)	4,000 lbs.

What did these numbers mean? If taken literally, a great deal. A rocket's velocity, or speed, is a function of its weight relative to its exhaust velocity. The classic rocket equation looks like this— $\Delta V = g_0 I_{sp} \ln w_I / w_F$—and indicates that for a rocket to reach orbit, its specific impulse, or I_{sp} (the time, in seconds, it takes one pound of propellant to produce one pound of thrust) must be very high, and its final weight (w_F, the weight of the empty rocket) must be extremely low compared to the weight of the rocket when full of fuel (w_I, the weight of the rocket on the launch pad).

A few of Gary's employees took these numbers at face value, among them Brian Binnie, who dutifully worked to find a way to include in the crew cabin climate controllers, pressure controllers, air scrubbers and oxygen controllers, fire-fighting equipment, ejection seats, data handling equipment, intercoms, flotation devices, flight avionics, crew members, cameras, recorders, candy bars, water, baggies, duct tape, and hygiene gear, all under 600 pounds. On the wall of his office he hung a bulletin board covered with F-18 and Desert Storm patches, a poster illustrating how the military develops space- and aircraft, a photograph of a pilot punching out of a crashing MIG, and a panoramic picture of the Kings Park golf course on which he'd grown up in Scotland. (When stationed on the *Midway*, he played its eighteen holes in his head if he couldn't sleep at night.) Several of Brian's military friends had gone on to become space shuttle commanders, but Brian hadn't gone that route. When it came time for him to apply to the astronaut corps, the *Challenger* had just exploded and nobody was sure when he might fly. Brian kept extremely fit and often used his hands to frame his field of vision, as if looking out a cockpit window. When asked what he thought about when designing a crew cabin, he said one word: "Survival."

But for most of Gary's employees these weight targets served primarily to add color to an elaborate rocket-building fantasy and thus were rather abstract. Rotary's first hire, Aleta Jackson, Rotary's "archivist," shared a small Mojave home with one of Rotary's founders, and one evening she told me her life story all in a rush. At age four she informed her father she was going to be "a spaceman." At age sixteen she ran away from home, got in a bad rural car accident, and was rescued by a McDonnell-Douglas man, who hired her on as a draftsperson for Project Gemini. Later she enrolled in the Indiana School of Technology, where, as the lone woman among 1,600 men, she was propositioned daily, met her first husband, and miscarried his child. Next she took a job editing the conservative space-military organ *The Journal of the High Frontier*, where she ran a picture of Gary's Phoenix rocket on the front cover of every issue for a year, and when people questioned her aesthetic judgment, she told them to fuck off. Now she lived in the desert preserving the memory of the Roton experience before it was complete. "Some people say Gary is ba-fucking-nanas, and I would say those people have no vision," she said. "I would not go to tea with them. Their souls are dust."

Bevin McKinney, Gary's original partner, was the only Rotary employee who fully understood both how the weight targets were derived and how far the company was from achieving them. Shaggy-haired, loose-limbed, enticingly soft-spoken with a low, gravelly voice, he had grown up an army brat in California and Germany. In college, he planned to study oceanography, but dropped that major in favor of art, realizing that oceanography is cold, wet, and muddy, and art is where all the pretty girls are. Later Bevin switched from art to naval architecture, and then dropped out of school altogether, earning a certificate from West Long College, School of Naval Architecture by Mail. He then spent ten years building crabbing boats. This gave Bevin a crucial distinction over Gary and Rotary's rivals: he had a taste for building functional vessels, and he knew how to build a manned ship that worked.

Bevin favored plain gray sweatshirts and relaxed-fit jeans, and spent his weekdays in White's Motel and his weekends in Sag Harbor, Washington, reading and rereading passages from *Moby Dick*. His office occupied a tight trailer corner in Building 31, the back wall of which he'd replaced with sliding glass windows looking out over the machine shop and garage. "I don't think there's maybe more than two or three people in this company who have the slightest notion of how much trouble we're going to have, how many things have to get done," Bevin said, untacking a poster-size Roton drawing. "As far as appearance goes, it looks about seventy percent designed, right? But that's only really ten percent in terms of what's actually going on. When you start seeing weird little bumps and things, that's when you know a vehicle is really maturing. Like this liquid oxygen pipe." He pointed with his index finger. "Nice pipe, easy to draw. But actually it's a really complicated thing to design. The billows, flexture, valves, how it attaches to the walls—it all has to be designed and engineered, a man-month's worth of work."

Bevin knew what he was getting into when he signed on to work with Gary. Gary, not Bevin, had a fondness for paraphrasing Bismarck: " 'One should not watch sausage or diplomacy being made.' The same might go for rockets." Gary, not Bevin, resembled the beautiful, fragile heroine of *A Streetcar Named Desire,* the half-mad Southern belle Blanche DuBois. Just as Blanche could not abide the sight of a stark bare lightbulb, Gary shuddered at the sight of his own screensaver, an image of the stars labeled with distances from Earth, a vision of the galaxy coldly harsh and hard-boiled, impossibly too far away. "I don't want realism. I want magic! Yes, yes, magic! I try to give that to people"—that was Blanche's, and Gary's, luminous tragic line. Bevin understood his partner when the two joined hands in 1996. Before founding the company Bevin and Gary discussed their respective roles.

Gary said, "I see my job as making sure the Roton gets built."

Bevin said, "Okay, that's great. I see my job as making sure the Roton gets designed first."

6

To live in a community of engineers is always to have your car running smoothly yet never to feel entirely at ease. It is to have conversations that never quite feel like conversations and to have relationships with machines that never quite feel like relationships with machines. One evening I asked Brent Eubanks, along with a few of his co-workers, if anyone might want to grab some dinner. "A social life?" Brent blurted out. "What a novel concept!" and so we all packed into the thermal-protection specialist's aging Jeep Cherokee and drove the thirty miles to the Outback restaurant in Palmdale.

On the ride down, Brent tugged at the pouch around his neck and said, reminiscent of Gary, "I believe in magic. Magic is the power to change things." Then he stuck his hand out the window and reported, "Air is just so weird." Brent had a way of talking—like calling poetry analog and engineering digital—that contained a certain poetry but to which nobody could possibly respond, so the car full of engineers stayed quiet except for the sounds of Rush, which Brent said was tied with Rusted Spoke for his favorite band. At the restaurant he charged into a discussion of whether caffeine was a drug, whether sugar was a drug, whether endorphins were a drug, whether running was a drug, until finally the thermal-protection specialist—to whom everybody listened, because he owned a house in Los Angeles and in his last job had made munitions-free weapons systems, like the stereo system with acoustic resonances that could knock down a wall—put the mania to a halt.

If running was a drug, then a pipe was a drug, and a pipe was clearly an input apparatus.

Brent nodded. Everyone agreed.

Dinner was a frenzy of eating—all clinking cutlery and chomping teeth—set off by the chilling stares of Palmdale youth, kids searching for meaning amid the skinhead gangs and wearying strip malls, the foreclosed neighborhoods torched in Hollywood movies (Mel Gibson and Danny Glover blew up an entire Palmdale development called the Legends in *Lethal Weapon 3*), and the water reclamation sites passed off as county parks. Recently one of Rotary's newest employees, a Lebanese-Canadian combustion specialist with a Stanford Ph.D., had spearheaded a misbegotten fishing trip to one of these non-attractions. His first Saturday in town, he drove his 1982 Cadillac to Christopher's house and convinced a few of the guys to take rods to the lakes above Palmdale, in the San Gabriel foothills. After consuming several bags of peanuts at the stagnant Lake Hughes without spotting a single fish, the group headed down to the stocked ponds—Lake Neil Armstrong, Lake Edwin "Buzz" Aldrin, and Lake Michael Collins—of Lancaster's Apollo Park. The text on a nearby space capsule replica worked very hard to equate the reclaimed waste water before us with Apollo 11, the first shot to the moon. "As man has conquered the unknown with the lunar flight of Apollo 11, he has brought water in the form of lakes for recreation to the arid desert." Spiders now crawled inside the capsule's fading interior. Nobody caught anything. Christopher drove the Cadillac a hundred miles an hour to get us home.

Our waitress's face formed a mask that seemed prepared for pain, wide eyes unblinking, never meeting ours. By meal's end, Brent had wolfed down his own whole twelve-ounce T-bone steak, plus four ounces of Christopher's and a good six ounces of mine. When the bill arrived, he attempted some differential calculus on the check.

"Let's just split it evenly," I suggested.

"You mean just divide the check by n?"

Brent stared, relieved and grinning. "I guess I'm sort of new at this," he said.

On the wall behind his desk Brent had taped an enlarged and Xeroxed section of *Creative Engineering,* a thin sherbet-green book on "blue-sky" design that Gary issued to all employees upon hiring them. The excerpt came from Chapter III, "The Challenge of Change":

Engineering problem-solving involves developing a way of thinking that is applicable to many kinds of problems, not just technical engineering problems. It is also a highly addictive activity. The designer begins by trying to find better ways of handling minor engineering problems. Sooner or later he focuses on larger solutions based on the rethinking of entire technological systems. Eventually, the design engineer looks for remedies to life's petty inconveniences, even though these problems may lie outside the strictly technical boundaries of engineering. Finally, a designer starts to think about the major problems of humankind, such as pollution, resource consumption, our tendency to treat others as less than human. . . .

Brent spent most days and nights at his computer, pulling unconsciously at the leather pouch around his neck and making imperceptibly small changes to rocket motor designs on his overlarge flickering screen. As a junior member of the propulsion team, Brent's primary responsibility was to redesign the 1.2-inch, stainless steel motor, the one that had failed in the first engine test. To do this, he not only had to worry about temperature and material, which had caused problems, but thrust, the force exerted by the engine's exhaust and specific impulse, or I_{sp}. Brent viewed engineering as a vocation, a practice, and he defined that practice as the process of making improvements by tiny increments, the exercise of endless tweaking, the art of turning what's broken, or what works suboptimally, or what does not yet exist, into its ideal. When fully engrossed in engineering, Brent described himself as "tapped into engineering Tao." His engineering philosophy stemmed from Robert Pirsig's *Zen and the Art of Motorcycle Maintenance:* "The Buddha, the Godhead, resides quite as comfortably in the circuits of a digital computer or the gears of a cycle transmission as he does at the top of a mountain or in the petals of a flower. To think otherwise is to demean the Buddha—which is to demean oneself."

7

Early in the fourth week of May, Gary placed a huge white model of an oceangoing freighter, with a small model Roton on its bow, on his Redwood Shores conference table. He sat beside the boat's stern wearing a bright green Hawaiian shirt, and flanking him on either side sat Rick Giarusso, Rotary's preppy, baby-faced, thirty-year-old CFO, and the envoy of a potential investor, an aging Canadian man in a pinstriped suit who spoke like a character out of *Glengarry Glen Ross*. "A lot of people get horny around Mr. L.," the envoy said, swiveling in his burgundy chair, stroking a hand along the freighter's hull. "He wanted to come down here but he took ill. He's a class act. You shouldn't have any trouble getting money. There's so much money out there it's crazy."

After Rick stood up and drew an elaborate diagram of the chunks of twenty and fifty million dollars he would raise in the coming months, Gary, sensing the presence of multiple fantasy lives, attempted to rein in his meeting. "I want to build the ship for two reasons," he said. "One, to regenerate revenue, and two, to launch from the equator. At the equator the earth rotates at a thousand feet per second so you get that extra boost. That's why the French launch the Ariane 5 from French Guyana. We considered Africa, but it's not politically feasible to launch from Liberia. There's no infrastructure, plus there're mosquitoes the size of aircraft."

Out of the $150 million needed to build the Roton, Rotary had raised thus far only $7.5 million, including the $1 million from Tom Clancy and the $5 million from Gold & Appel, the venture capital fund managed by Walt Anderson. Now Gary was proposing to buy a 60,000-deadweight-ton ship. "This ship itself will cost $18 to $25 million, and then we'll need to modify the cargo holds, one into a hangar and at least one more into satellite storage, and that could run another $60 million, but I could be twenty percent off."

The envoy pulled on his lapels. "What flag do you plan to sail this ship under?"

"Any flag you want," Gary said, jocular. "It could be done as a subsidiary joint venture. The time to build the ship is just about two years. The other possibility is to build the ship custom, but that's pricey—$80 to $90 million. The only thing we need is a stable platform, and enough hangar space to keep everything out of the wind and spray." Gary handed out 8½ × 11 glossy illustrations of the Roton. They looked like photographs. "We've made a few modifications since the last time you saw it. We've moved the propellant tank forward, which makes it more stable at liftoff."

The envoy chuckled to himself. "Heh-heh. You put the rocket up in the morning and you bring it back down and it's fresh and brand new—now there's a hell of a deal. That's a significant advantage. I think you're on to a winner." He shook the model, jerkily, like a sports fan. "I think my man might put ten million into the ship. I don't think he's your man for the rocket, but I think he'll like the ship. This is a beautiful project. Beautiful. Heh-heh. This is almost better than sex."

In addition to commissioning the model of this $80-million ship, Gary hired a Los Angeles architect to design a seventy-foot-tall high-bay building in which to garage his soon-to-be-fabricated Roton ATV, and then, because drawings were being made, he bespoke a 10,000-square-foot low bay and a 21,000-square-foot engineering suite fronted by a sheer wall of steel and glass. The groundbreaking for this complex took place on the third Friday in June, and on the morning of the event Building 31 hangar felt like a high school gym before a football banquet—workbenches covered with rented white tablecloths, cubed cheese on plastic trays. Anne Hudson pushed around a cart piled with white polo shirts embroidered with the Rotary Rocket logo. "Hey Johnny! Hey Phish!" she screamed, her voice rising over the hangar's clanging swamp coolers. "Get your asses over here. Don't you want no stinkin' shirts?"

As Anne described it, "This isn't international, this is just for the local guys." And when she finished outfitting her husband's employees (most of whom donned the Rotary T-shirt over whatever they had on), one of the secretaries—a former Denny's waitress who upon learning that Rotary provided health insurance for her children broke down and cried—approached and said, "Don't the guys look great?"

Anne leaned her weight against a trailer, relaxed her maternal face. "I guess everybody has something different that makes this all seem real. For me it was picking out color palettes. I didn't think we were at that stage yet, but I'm told that if we want the high bay to have painted girders, we need to order the paint right now."

Despite the 105-degree heat, by eleven o'clock all Kern County turned out to celebrate—Roger White, Roger White's daughter, Cheryl, Burt Rutan, Burt's brother, Dick, and Miss Mojave 1998. At the construction site, just behind the airport's control tower, a compact test site worker named Ken tapped Gary on the shoulder, saying, "Gary, I'd like you to meet my wife." Ken had already lived in Mojave for three months, but his wife had just arrived, reluctant to leave her home in Utah, a teaching job she loved, a close-knit group of Mormon friends who'd seen her through the death of a child. "We just bought a house," he said to his boss, nodding. "I just thought you might want to know."

After the speeches, the gold spray-painted shovels, and the cheese and champagne in the hangar, the Rotary crew—inflated by the attention, unsure what it meant—retired out to the test site to cook hot dogs and burgers and shoot off a potato gun. The gun consisted of a yard of medium-gauge PVC tubing, its leading edge sharpened, and a flint and propane bulb at the rear. A small crowd bunched around one of the company pickups, the ground speckled with the confetti of pink potato skins, the air smelling fresh and starchy, and, from the propane, like dead rats. Johnny dug into the bag of new Bliss and shoved a potato down the PVC pipe with a broom handle, stripping off its skin. He filled up the bulb with gas and set the cylinder against his thigh. He launched his payload into the desert, the potato rising through the air with a hollow, plastic *thwump*.

■   ■   ■

The following weekend, Christopher hosted a barbecue in Cal City, the third largest city in California in terms of area, the eleventh largest in the United States, population 9,000. Settled in 1958 when Nat Mendelsohn bought 80,000 acres of the Boron Valley and started selling homes for $9,659 each, the town was a misfiring of 1960s real estate speculation. Whole downtown blocks still offered nothing but Joshua trees and creosote bush. Several would-be-neighborhoods on cul-de-sacs featured only one house. To prepare for the party, Christopher removed the lithium nitrate (a bomb-making material) from his oven, screwed the lids on all his chemical-filled mason jars, and asked the thermal-protection specialist to tend the grill. Following this, for a few glorious minutes, flames spilled from the grill's top and bottom. Then they burned out. Christopher scurried into his garage and returned with a bag of ammonium nitrate, the fertilizer used by Timothy McVeigh in the Oklahoma City bombing. The fire flared, then died again. This time Christopher ran inside and returned with a bag of lithium oxide. The lithium oxide was a prized possession. Christopher had pinched it during a stint of coaching peewee football when one of his kids had required a cold pack for a twisted ankle. Christopher took the pack home and evaporated out the powder.

"I love it," Christopher screamed, manic, drizzling the sugar-like grains on the coals and replacing the black dome. The fire flared, then fizzled once more. Finally, the tawny-skinned secretary from the test site, the only other woman at the party, set down her beer and pulled on a grill mitt. She slid open the Weber's top and bottom vents, both of which had been closed.

Christopher lit off some homemade fireworks and an M-80, the last burst rendering the world a negative image of itself, the bougainvillea black against the white night sky, the grill a pale globe staked to the ground. We all ate charred chicken while sitting on Christopher's living room carpet, struggling to make sense of what we were doing here by discussing the greatest rocket moments in our lives. Norman Mailer, who was paid a million dollars to write *Of a Fire on the Moon* (1970), a book about the Apollo program, had called our space ambition "the spookiest venture in history." "He hardly knew," he admitted, writing of himself in the third person, "whether the space program was the noblest expression of the twentieth century or the quintessential statement of our fundamental insanity." Between Kennedy's speech and the moon landing the country endured four assassinations, Vietnam, the burning of black ghettos, hippies, drugs, student uprisings, the Democratic Convention in Chicago, the New York school strike, and the sexual revolution. My prime contribution to the conversation was talking about the day I sat by the humid lagoon on Cape Kennedy, enduring the long launch delays and drinking sweet tea. I knew how much space meant to so many people. Still, when the *Discovery* rose up on its pillar of fire, I felt ill-prepared. The rocket rose slowly, majestically, out of the swampy air, shedding spent external tanks like sweaters in spring. I found the sight deeply inspiring and achingly, existentially sad. We all remained on the ground, sweat-soaked and smothered in sunscreen, while six shuttle astronauts had been able to leave.

Only one representative of Gary's gang of old-timers turned up at Christopher's that evening, and throughout the party he lay flat against the floor, staring at the spiders on the ceiling, hands folded atop his paunch. Wild-haired and appealing, he'd been engaged once, eighteen years ago, but hadn't had the courage for romance since. When it came his turn to speak, he exhaled loudly several times—a halting laugh. "You know," he said, "I was really into rockets for fourteen years before I started to realize there were other things in life." He stared at Christopher and Brent, both already into rockets for that long, both roughly half his age. "You know what getting a rocket to work is like? The reward is power, male power in particular. You can feel the thrust of this thing. It's releasing energy and emitting all this hot fluid. It's going to stage eventually. . . ." The room fell silent, ashamed. "I mean, you ever met a woman rocket nerd before? You get really nervous before each test, there's the chance that you're going to fail, and then afterwards you want to relax and go have a cigarette. It's a mistake to let yourself think that rockets are all that's important. You don't want to be on your deathbed thinking about the Saturn V."

8

Anyone who has plumbed his own psychology knows that the capacity for fantasy can lead to salvation as well as to demise. Fantasies free us and damn us too, for while dreams taken a short way are magically cathartic, gone too far they consign us to delusion. As is booze for the human heart—soothing in small doses, ravaging in large, cruelly difficult for some to resist—so too can be science fiction. For while in the real world we are flawed, small, lonely, yearning for escape, in science fiction we are galactically significant, careening through wormholes, freed from the body, the flesh. And, conveniently, we need not dismiss this as daydream; we're on firm "scientific" ground. Perhaps for this reason science fiction has a history of being both addictive and dangerous. (The genre is a chance illustration of Sol LeWitt's *Sentences on Conceptual Art, #5:* "Irrational thoughts should be followed absolutely and logically.") Shoko Asahara, the half-blind guru behind Japan's Aum Shinrikyo cult who manufactured biological weapons to take over the world, was inspired by Isaac Asimov's *Foundation* series. Charles Manson modeled himself on Valentine Michael Smith, the rich, powerful superlover in Robert Heinlein's science fiction bestseller *Stranger in a Strange Land.*

Science fiction histories typically begin not with Plato or *The Birds* of Aristophanes or *The Odyssey*—all of which, arguably, fall into the genre—but with the A.D. 160 *True History* of Lucian of Samosata, the first written account of interplanetary travel. The text starts in a rhetoric weirdly similar to Gary's: "I shall at least say one thing true when I tell you that I lie, and shall hope to escape the general censure by acknowledging that I mean to speak not a word of truth throughout." Next on the historical docket are Kepler's *Somnium* (1634), Bishop Francis Godwin's pro-Copernican romance, *Man in the Moone, or A Discourse of a Voyage Thither by Domingo Gonsales* (1638), and Cyrano de Bergerac's *Voyage dans la lune* (1650), in which, after an abortive experiment with bottles of dew, our hero reaches the moon in a chariot powered, for the first time in history, by rockets. Notably omitted from the traditional science fiction annals is Shakespeare's *The Tempest,* the tale of an eccentric scientist-recluse, his beautiful daughter, the early mutant Caliban, and, in the words of Kingsley Amis, a major science fiction fan, the "anthropomorphised mobile scanner," Ariel.

The canon then moves through Swift's *Gulliver's Travels* and Bacon's *New Atlantis,* stopping midway at Mary Shelley's *Frankenstein.* To Poe next (though grudgingly), and finally on to the modern forefathers: Jules Verne and H. G. Wells. Verne, at last, produces the mechanized utopia, concerning himself with technology—in Wells's words, with the "actual possibilities of invention and discovery," evidenced by long scientific lectures—whereas Wells just spews a few lines of pseudoscience patter and fires his characters out of the atmosphere and on their way. Together, Verne and Wells liberated science fiction from both the rigors of science (thanks to Wells) and those of literature too (thanks to Verne), making way for the genre's contemporary cohorts, many of whom crank out books at a rate faster than one a year.

Throughout modern history, the membrane between science fiction and actual rocketry has proven almost wholly permeable. Rocketry paterfamilias Konstantin Tsiolkovsky once said, "My interest in space travel was first aroused by the famous writer of fantasies, Jules Verne. Curiosity was followed by serious thought." The filmmaker Fritz Lang later commissioned Tsiolkovsky's successor, Hermann Oberth, to advise him on the set of *Die Frau im Mond* (1929). Oberth, in turn, influenced Wernher von Braun, the result being an on-screen spaceship that very strongly resembled the Saturn V. "It's hard to tell, given the history of the movie, whether fiction influenced science or science influenced fiction," writes the space historian Howard McCurdy in his book *Space and the American Imagination.* Von Braun promoted his multistage rockets in *Collier's* magazine. He also collaborated on a three-part Disney series linked to the Tomorrowland theme park, at the center of which towered an eighty-foot needle-nosed rocket designed by von Braun himself.

In the 1960s, while American popular and counterculture broadly trounced technology—the trigger-happy insanity of Stanley Kubrick's *Dr. Strangelove* (1964), the simian nightmare in Franklin Schaffner's *Planet of the Apes* (1968)—space travel still culled utopian visions, most notably Kubrick's next offering, *2001: A Space Odyssey* (1968). *2001* depicted space as a rhapsody of spiritual awakening (and featured, incidentally, a space shuttle four years before Nixon directed NASA to start building one). Kubrick's aesthetics shape space enthusiasts' up to the present, as I experienced firsthand in April 1998 at the Space Access Convention in Scottsdale, Arizona. There, among the zebra prints and squawking parrots at the Safari Hotel, a large man handed me a pamphlet for Space Island Resort, from which, I was told, one could watch sunrise sixteen times a day. "You understand," he said, flipping to a picture of a sleek modernist spa fashioned out of spent space shuttle external fuel tanks, "this is not a hobby. I do not want to *go* to space. I want to *move*."

The Space Access Society was the brainchild of Henry Vanderbilt, a marginally employed ex–computer game programmer with thick, knotted sideburns, a 130-pound Akita named Rufo, and a habit of spending weekends in handmade suits of medieval armor. Every year, since 1989, he'd sent out invitations and lined up lecturers—Gary always among them—and spacers had trekked in from as far as Japan to spend three days swapping rocket drawings and discussing extraterrestrial life. At the far end of the hotel, in an outbuilding, a slope-shouldered woman with hip-length hair hunched behind the convention registration desk. She eyed me warily, as a local might a tourist, certain I was in the wrong place.

"Can I help you?"

My name was on her list.

"Oh—we must really be branching out. You just . . ." She drummed her fingers on her clipboard. "You just look like such a mundane."

Mundane is science fiction vernacular for those humans so tedious as to be interested only in the extant, no-imagination-required world. *SF,* not *sci fi,* is the proper abbreviation, and the slope-shouldered woman shared her house with fifty-one cats and six golden retrievers. She and her equally fanatical husband spent nearly every weekend at SF cons (as opposed to space cons, like this one), and they claimed they could spot their fellow fen (the SF plural of *fan,* a derivative of *men*) in third-world markets and airport baggage claims with 99 percent accuracy. Reluctantly, she handed me a Space Access packet and badge. A few young men in thin ponytails and black T-shirts walked past without hassle. The woman smiled tightly. "Maybe we'll have you looking like a convert by the time you get out."

Gary, like almost everybody else who worked at Rotary, had grown up in the science fiction world among the fen. His favorite books were Larry Niven and Jerry Pournelle's *The Mote in God's Eye* and Poul Anderson's *The Earth Book of Stormgate,* and he believed that science fiction taught its readers that "there is no end to accomplishments" and that "the future is yours to create." He believed that adults who had not read science fiction as children had "far more self-doubt" and were "far more skeptical" about what an individual or a society could do. Jaws dropped in Mojave when I first admitted that I hadn't read Heinlein or Bradbury. Or Asimov either. On came an avalanche of well-thumbed paperbacks, people explaining, with generous hearts, that I could not understand them unless I read this one or that. Embarrassingly, I tried to return the favor, extending copies of my own dog-eared favorites—James Salter's *Light Years,* Joan Didion's *Slouching Toward Bethlehem*—which people politely accepted and completely ignored. Why? As Alexei and Cory Panshin explain in their fannish manifesto, *SF in Dimension,* "mimetic fiction"— that is, realistic fiction—is "a negative drag on literature." Moreover, "SF which rejects its freedom to be positive is as big a bummer as mimetic fiction."

In the Safari's mauve, windowless meeting hall, a rabbinically bearded zoology professor stood at the podium delivering a cross between a physics lecture, the Sermon on the Mount, and the State of the Union address. "Beware of research people," he solemnly told the crowd. "Their goal is not transportation, which is yours. . . . Challenge the gospel of liquid hydrogen, doubts have been expressed of late." Heads bobbed with the dreaminess of familiarity, the two hundred men and ten women nodding off like children to a bedtime story or parishioners at a Latin mass. "Escape velocity is eight kilometers per second. . . . Remember the major criterion for getting to space is not altitude but speed."

Switching on the overhead projector, the rabbi drew a diagram—first a circle, which he said represented a planet such as Earth, and then, off the planet's surface, a series of curves, each starting at twelve o'clock and arching clockwise around. The smallest curve arched in a parabola from twelve o'clock to one o'clock—a bullet, the rabbi said, shot out of a gun, traveling a short way around the earth before it hit the ground. The next, from twelve to two, a bullet flying slightly farther. Then finally a less steep curve, resulting in a circle looping all the way around.

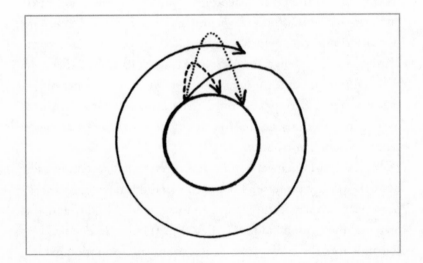

This last bullet had gone into orbit, become a sputnik, a satellite, a moon. The concept, he said, came from Isaac Newton's *Principia* (as did the original drawing above). The rabbi turned off the projector and clasped his hands under his chin. "Reaching orbit is easy," he quipped. "It's just like throwing yourself at the ground and missing."

Gary, of course, had spent most of his adult life throwing himself at the ground and hitting. Part of the trouble was that he had long been obsessed with building a single-stage-to-orbit spaceship: fill up the gas tank, go to space, come back down, fill up the gas tank again. The trouble is that a single-stage-to-orbit rocket is like a single-dip ice cream cone—one unit, one engine. A two-stage-to-orbit rocket, much easier to build, is like a double-dip cone—two units, two thrusts. With the single-stage rocket, the engine fires, and the rocket goes however fast it goes. With the two-stage—typically a large rocket with a small rocket attached to its nose—the large bottom rocket fires first. Then, when it has reached its peak speed and its fuel is almost gone, the second rocket fires, accelerating faster still, effectively adding the thrusts of the two engines together. (The Saturn V was a three-stage rocket. The space shuttle has two and a half stages.)

After the rabbi's lecture, Gary filed with the rest of the listeners out into a hallway, joining the suited reps from Pratt & Whitney and the booths explaining space tethers. From the throng, a man thrust at me a business card: MITCHELL "MITCH" BURNSIDE CLAPP, PRESIDENT FOR NOW, PIONEER ROCKETPLANE, saying, "Might be nice for you to follow somebody who's actually going to fly. . . ."

Mitch, working hard to separate himself from the masses, told me he'd recently taken over the helm of Pioneer from Robert

Zubrin, whose excessive Mars enthusiasm had been deemed a fundraising liability. He had a wholly round face, a Charlie Brown haircut, a smile deviously self-assured. Within minutes he'd found occasion to note that he was fluent in Russian, wrote music in his spare time, designed his own house, baked his own bread, and built a swing set for his girls. He'd earned four degrees from Harvard and M.I.T. in only four years. His call name as an Air Force test pilot had been Fever, as in too many degrees. While in the service, Mitch had established a reputation for himself in spacer circles, proving in his precocious style that (a) it's possible to produce materials light enough to build a single-stage rocket, and (b) those materials are as common as the alloy in a can of Budweiser. Now he glanced down the corridor and snickered at a group of spacers utterly lost in a debate about contraptions for facilitating sex in zero gravity. "I don't want to turn eighty," he said, "and say, 'Hey, I could have been a contender, I could have been somebody.' "

Across the room, Gary chatted easily with the widow of G. Harry Stine, the recently deceased father of model rocketry, author of *Halfway to Anywhere,* and inventor of the psychokinetic energy wheel, a device which looked much like a Roton rotor and which, Stine claimed, could be turned by focusing the mind alone. Mitch kept talking, smug. "The Russian guys solved my combustion problems ten years ago. I have two terrifyingly intelligent children and a beautiful, pregnant wife. I read great books. I'm happier than I ever expected to be. The happiest man is he who has the most interesting thoughts."

His voice sunk to a whisper just before he walked away. "Me," he said, "I'm a nonbeliever. I'm just a guy who likes to fly cool planes all the way up to space—the sky turns black, hey, there's the moon. There's a difference between having a vision or a dream and having a religion. All these other people are here out of delusions or frustrations. Or else they're part of a cult."

Sunday morning the sun rose fast and uncivilly bright over the Safari's green lawn. Gary had been slotted to speak at eight A.M.—an inducement to get everybody out of bed, or so the event's organizer hoped—but at seven-thirty, the only movement at the al fresco buffet came from the organizer himself, slicing mini-bagels, and from his enormous dog, Rufo. Gary sat alone on the white cement pool deck, picking at scrambled eggs. "The problem is," he muttered, "at eight A.M. I don't have *any* interesting things to say." He'd soaked his Mephistos on the watered grass. His cup and saucer rattled as he raised them to sip.

The prior afternoon a group of Rotary employees, minus Gary, had driven out for a swim and early supper at the home of the CFO Rick's father. The host had repeated all of our names, shaking hands firmly as we walked in. He then led us through his new house to his backyard, where, against a backdrop of rippled dunes, he'd fenced in a tennis court-size patch of sand.

Gary declined to attend due to growing tension—neither he nor Rick had raised much money—and around the pool, conversation turned to where everyone thought would be better to retire: the moon or Mars. "Who's nicer," Rick asked, starting into his pro–space colonization syllogism, "a New Yorker or an Iowa farmer? The planet needs a safety valve, that much is clear. And we can't just build a colony in Antarctica or under the deep sea because you'll have to deal with international law, visas, vaccines, border patrols. It's not a pure situation. Outside forces will still be imposing rules."

Most of the ideas on the deck spun off Robert Zubrin's Mars manifesto and the writings of the turn-of-the-century American historian Frederick Jackson Turner. In 1893, Turner argued that in the presence of an open frontier, people are both forced and free to come up with new ideas, both technological and social, and in the absence of an open frontier, the world becomes trampled, overcrowded, spoiled, and bleak, with an increasing hostility to new ideas, outsiders, immigrants, and so forth. "There'll be nothing rarer in a Mars colony," Zubrin had once explained to me, "than human labor time, and the labor shortage will drive a freedom of necessity, and that in turn would provide that 'coarseness of strength combined with acuteness and inquisitiveness; that practical, inventive turn of mind . . . that restless nervous energy; that dominant individualism' of which Turner wrote a hundred years ago."

The basic idea, as argued here, was that life would feel better, freer, off the earth's surface. "I'm not somebody who can just sit around doing nothing, not for very long anyway," explained Jeff Greason, the overlarge head of Rotary's propulsion team. "At the same time, I'd like to—there's a lot of theoretical problems I'd like to work on in gravitational physics, I enjoy playing strategy and role-playing games. Over the past couple of years this feeling has grown up in the back of my brain that if I leave the planet, just staying alive comfortably would be good enough. I wouldn't have to keep looking around for something to do. If I had time to take away from the life support system for leisure, I could just do that. It would be a sufficiently important accomplishment to be able to show that people can live off Earth's surface. Whenever I just wanted to sit down, read books, watch TV, do whatever it is, that would be okay, I'd be doing it on Mars."

By dusk, consensus was that Mars would make a better residence—too few natural resources on the moon; you'd have to be a computer programmer there. The CFO's father never quite warmed to the issue. When asked his opinion he just slipped off his sandals and his white golf shirt and dove into the confines of his square blue pool.

By eight o'clock the following morning, the conference room was filled with spacers, several wearing PHOENIX R.I.P. T-shirts, a tribute to a previous rocket of Gary's that never flew. Handsome and composed, Gary stood at the podium with a microphone clipped to his shirt collar and a cell phone clipped to his belt. "I think the most important virtue," he began slowly, drawing in his crowd, "for anyone starting a business in commercial space transportation is persistence, and it is the most underrated virtue in the universe."

He tapped the tips of his fingers together in front of his nose, compulsive yet calm. "This virtue was illustrated last night when a few of our colleagues and I decided to go out to dinner. It's kind of a ritual for Friday night at these Space Access conferences. We did that three years ago, and went to a very nice microbrewery with Asian fusion cuisine, right over at the mall. But last year, when we decided to go back to the same place, we were rather disappointed to find it had been demolished. So we found a very nice Italian restaurant across the way, and last night we wandered over there again, and to our chagrin, that Italian restaurant had turned into a video store. So we found a Southwestern place nearby. And I really didn't have the heart to tell the waitress what I'll tell you, the secret of my success: I'll be back next year, but you won't."

After a brief chuckle, Gary glossed over the challenges before him for the coming year—"one, financing; two, regulation; and three, technology, in that order"—and then he said, in a self-satisfied tone, "Let's just say this talk contains the standard amount of propaganda. The more money that comes in, the more impossible it becomes to talk about what's really going on." For instance, about the crew, he said, "We like to describe the Roton as being piloted rather than manned. Unmanned vehicles have failure rates two thousand times higher than manned vehicles. And this isn't Spam in a can we're talking about here. What I'm talking about is a pilot capable of flight during all phases." About the engine: "Rotary's design philosophy is 'Build at All Costs.' We're already building engines out at our test facility in Mojave. People have the mistaken impression that rocket engines are difficult things to build, and that's not true at all. They're no harder to build than jet engines. We just don't build as many of them." About Scaled Composites' use of carbon fibers: "People get all excited about putting LOX in organic or quasi-organic containers. I don't know what all the fuss is all about. It's been tested, and it works fine. I'm thinking about taking my Remington 700 down to Mojave on the Fourth of July and firing an incendiary round at the tank, just to see if I can *make* it catch fire."

Gary also announced, for the first time publicly, that he was building down in Mojave his full-scale Roton prototype—his landing-gear demonstrator, the ATV—and he invited everybody to the desert the following spring to see the rocket rolled out. Shouts rang out for details; Gary obliged. The crew cabin would seat two for now, four to six in the future. The N, or registration, number on the vehicle would be 0707, Robert Heinlein's birthday. The rocket itself, the Roton-C, had grown slightly larger than originally projected due to the increased size of communications satellites, but he and Bevin now planned to fabricate smaller transportation-only models as well, perhaps for the space tourism industry. Rotary Rocket would fly and service the first few Rotons, then shift to a manufacturing-only role. Each Roton would be guaranteed for a hundred flights. Gary would not fly on the first.

After twenty-five minutes, Gary unclipped his microphone and placed it on the stand. "I do have a copy of our video. . . ," he said, removing his reading specs. "But I think most of you have seen it before."

"Run it!"

"Run it!"

"Run it!"

"Really?" Gary strained.

"YES!"

"Run it again, Gary!"

"Run for it, Gary!"

"All right," Gary said, and as spectators from the back of the room spilled into the front aisle, he pulled a cassette from his canvas briefcase and slid it into the waiting VCR. Again, the Enya-like music, the Roton on its launch cart, the two uniformed pilots climbing aboard. Just as the rocket started to rise, Gary paused the tape. "To remind you," he said, "this video contains a very large amount of disinformation. The engine doesn't work like that. The rotors don't deploy like that. The vehicle doesn't look like that. Almost nothing that you'll see is correct."

9

A peculiar calm settled over Mojave with the knowledge that Scaled Composites was building the Roton. The town still had no library, no movie theater, no decent restaurant, and no way to spend time outside, and yet its residents viewed it with pride, as a hotbed of aviation, and everyone pointed to Burt Rutan as evidence of this.

Burt lived in a nearly windowless, largely underground, pyramid-shaped home of his own design, because, as he reasoned, "I see enough of Mojave just driving home." After graduating third in his class from the California Polytechnic Institute in 1965, he tested aircraft at Edwards Air Force Base. Then he established the Rutan Aircraft Factory down the road in Mojave, selling plans and kits for home-built planes. But Rutan Aircraft Factory led to too much time sitting across courtroom tables from the families of people who crashed them, so Burt founded Scaled Composites, a company committed to designing strange, new, limit-pushing aircraft like Voyager, which Burt's brother, Dick—a Vietnam-seasoned combat pilot—and Dick's petite ex-girlfriend, Jeanna Yeager, flew around the world on a single tank of fuel. Burt, Dick, and Jeanna conceived the idea in the Mojave Inn on a napkin. Burt sketched an extremely long wing, two engines, a central crew cabin, and a canard wing. He called this design #76. It became the seventy-sixth entry in his notebook.

The primary challenges of the Voyager were figuring out how to store the 9,000 pounds of fuel required to fly 28,000 statute miles without disastrously affecting control, weight, and balance, and how to build valves simple enough to operate during such a long and demanding flight. One competitor for the round-the-world title crashed his plane at the Mojave airport while Burt was working on his, and the day Dick and Jeanna took off in the Voyager no one felt sure they would return. The flight was mostly over water, and in Burt's words, "If you had to put it down, you die." But return they did, nine days later, becoming the first pilots to leave an airport and return to the same airport, without stopping, without refueling, and without turning around. Back on the ground, eighteen gallons of fuel left in the tank, Dick informed his brother of the plane's smoky cockpit, electrical arcing, and failing seals. But Burt never fixed them, and nobody flew the Voyager again. The vehicle hangs in its flawed condition in the Smithsonian today.

Scaled Composites occupies a drab warren of buildings on the Mojave airport flight line, and its public face, its lobby (many of its hangars are off-limits to visitors), presents a shrine to achievement, a mirror opposite of Gary's temple to failure. The walls display an ever-growing array of paintings depicting Burt's fantastical armada, each plane a monument to the premise that you can make exquisite aircraft out of carbon fiber and glue, hardening that glue with hairdryers. The tableaus are all set over the famous eighteenth hole of the Cypress Point golf course, and above the sea, crags, and greens you can see the Boomerang (twin-hulled and twin-engined, without bilateral symmetry), the Freewing Scorpion UAV (looking as if someone had chopped off the tail section and folded up the nose forty-five degrees), the Microlight, the Starship 1, the Predator, the Scarab, the Triumph, the ARES, the Pond Racer, the B-2 bomber, the Pegasus, the ATTT, the Visionaire Business Jet, the NASA X-38 Crew Return Vehicle, the Hunter RPV (Remotely Piloted Vehicle), the Searcher RPV, the Raptor, and the DC-X, and, on the golf cart path, the GM Ultralite car. Framed magazine covers picturing the same vehicles line a short narrow hallway. Trophies won for their creation fill a mahogany case.

The Roton ATV was the largest airframe Scaled Composites had ever signed on to build, and its first helicopter, and that summer work began in a tin-roofed shed where a five-axis, numerically controlled, single-armed gantry carved molds, or "plugs," out of 35 × 15 × 5-foot blocks of Styrofoam. Scaled's process for fabricating the ATV, like its process of fabricating just about anything—airplanes, cars, hot air balloons, missiles, surfboards, any structure that needed to be light and strong, and in a complex shape—consisted of five steps.

1. Chisel a plug (a positive, or male, form).
2. Use the plug to lay up a tool (a negative, or female, form).
3. Use the tool to lay up a part (a positive form again).
4. Tape the parts into components.
5. Integrate the components into a vehicle.

The single-armed gantry's giant computerized limb moved up and down, front and back, side to side, its wrist bent and hand swiveled, working deliberately, chiseling blanks, producing a blizzard of plastic dandruff, and emitting a soothing, sucking whir. The foam weighed five pounds per cubic foot, the same grade of foam used for floating lakeborne docks. Gary's ATV had six main components—the LOX tank, the nitrogen tank, the payload bay (for satellite storage), the crew cabin, the igloo (for housing the rotor blades), and the Frisbee (substitute for the engine). Scaled cut these components as needed into halves, quarters, or eighths, so that the gantry could cut the plugs out of the standard-size billets of foam.

Once cut, Scaled hauled the foam plugs into a clean room, a vaulting workshop with sheer white walls, vast concrete floors, and counters exceptionally well appointed with sandpaper, latex gloves, Popsicle sticks, sheet plastic, rolls of unidirectional and bidirectional cloth, peel ply, prepreg, brushes, T-squares, and paper buckets. A huge triptych of posters—supplied by Gary—provided inspiration: a Roton shooting straight up on a pillar of fire, a Roton floating above the earth, and a Roton with its rotors extended, drifting back down. (The posters additionally inspired Scaled employees to shoot a spoof stop-action animation, with a rocket made out of LEGOs.) Here, under the high fluorescent lights, men in white bunny suits and green latex gloves laid sheets of carbon fiber over Styrofoam plugs. Then they smoothed buckets of resin into the fabric. The process resembled the making of a plaster of Paris cast.

Less than a hundred yards away from the clean room stood Burt's latest sensation, the Proteus. The plane was widely rumored to be the first stage of his X Prize vehicle, and it was strong, pure, and hollow-looking, like the skeleton of a large, genteel bird. Named after the Greek shape-changing god, the Proteus could stay aloft eighteen hours with its tail-first design, its twin tailbooms, and its wings spanning ninety-five feet. Burt had designed the vehicle to be chameleon-like, to take advantage of various markets and dreams. One could attach satellite dishes to the bottom, providing ultrafast communications to underlying cities. Or, with slightly more hassle, one could attach rocket boosters, possibly launching payloads, even passenger pods, to orbit.

In 1975 Burt had revolutionized aircraft design by building a wing for his private plane out of urethane foam and unidirectional fiberglass. Traditionally, planes had been built out of aluminum alloy, or, in rare cases, steel. But while metals are strong, they are also heavy, a significant disadvantage given that one of the prime metrics in the aerospace industry is the wet mass fraction—the ratio of the mass of fuel in a vehicle to the mass of everything else one is attempting to lift off. A commercial airliner at departure typically has a wet mass fraction of about fifty—half the mass on the runway is fuel. At liftoff, the space shuttle has a wet mass fraction of around seventy-five; 75 percent of the mass at liftoff is fuel. For a single-stage rocket going orbital, the conventional wisdom is that one needs to get the wet mass fraction up over ninety or ninety-two, meaning the airframe must be primarily a light, fuel-filled balloon. The best wet mass fraction anyone has ever achieved on a functional, single-stage passenger-carrying vehicle is seventy-five: that was Burt Rutan, for his Voyager. Composite vehicles are about 20 percent lighter than aluminum ones, so Gary found Burt's services extremely enticing.

A composite is defined as a combination of materials differing in consistency and form, typically a binder or matrix, and a reinforcement. Wood is a composite—long fibers of cellulose held together with lignin—as is reinforced concrete—steel bars surrounded by cement. For their density, composites are extremely strong. Imagine, for example, a mud brick—capable of carrying a lot of weight but easy to break by bending—and a length of straw—strong against stretching, but no resistance to being crumpled up. Now imagine embedding the straw into the mud brick. The result, adobe, resists both squeezing and tearing, withstands both compressive and tensile loads.

The most common composite in the aerospace industry is carbon fabric embedded in resin. The resin hardens, or cures, at a specific temperature, sometimes room temperature, and the setting process is irreversible—the resin won't soften again if exposed to high heat. (The entire ATV was room-temperature-cured, except for the ellipsoid nitrogen tank, which had to be fabricated in a climate-controlled cold room—67 degrees, 40 percent humidity, heaven in Mojave—using the stronger, more durable "prepreg," a textile pre-impregnated with resin.) Carbon fabric/resin composites wear well, don't break, and can be easily molded into precise mathematical shapes. For these reasons, throughout the summer, the ATV clean room resembled a sort of arts-and-crafts playground, cluttered with scissors, fabric, resin, and tape, with scaffolding hovering above the tooling. Each morning one crew would cut a length of cloth, place it on a large steel table, pour on a layer of resin, squeegee the excess off, and then drag the soaked fabric onto the mold, careful to smooth out the wrinkles. A second crew would then climb on the scaffolding, lie on their stomachs or dangle from their knees, and stroke in still more resin. So the "wet layups" progressed, day after day, week after week, from plug to tool to part, until all the ATV's halves, quarters, and eighths stood in a pile in the corner, a heaping fragile mountain of sawed-off, open casts.

Marti and Brian observed Scaled's progress closely, the only Rotary employees to do so, walking across the burning black pavement several times a week, often to discuss the details of the ATV's crew cabin, currently a mound of curved slabs on the clean-room floor. To save money, Brian had recently scoured the infernally hot aerospace warehouses around Edwards Air Force Base, turning up one of the ATV's two required crash seats secondhand for about one-tenth the price of buying a seat new. Now he and Marti stood in the cavernous hangar discussing with the Scaled chief how to attain peripheral vision while still sitting at a safe distance back from the round portal door. Brian held up his right hand and moved it slowly across his field of view, chest squarely forward, as if in a five-point harness. Marti asked, "Can we install the seats tilted forward fifteen degrees?"

"It'd be easier just to tilt the floor," the Scaled chief chuckled in response. "We also can't think of enough switches to fill the control panel. We're trying to keep the cabin really, really clear and simple, so you guys won't snag when this thing tips over and you're running out the front door."

10

In the tight squeeze of 110-degree heat, Christopher hauled the centrifuge out to the test site for the second time. The machine had been designed to test spinning rocket engines, and it looked like a steroid-addled discus thrower: barrel helicopter transmission torso, overstretched cylindrical arms, and purple-painted stainless steel legs. Johnny Hernandez, the skateboard punk, helped Christopher mount it in its three-planed corner of reinforced concrete and then walked over near the whirl stand pit to watch; a new silver arrowhead was pierced through his lip, his boots coming apart from kicking too many rocks. "Damn damn damn damn damn," he said, "that thing is hauling ass." The centrifuge spun up to 100 RPM, less than one-seventh of the 720 RPM it would eventually need to go. The test failed—too much wobble in the arms. As he left, Christopher stuck his chest out the window of his green Toyota pickup, weaving tight circles around Johnny. "You're the champion! You're the champion! You're the champion!" he shouted. Johnny stood in the center, spinning very slowly, head tilted back, arms stretched wide, palms turned up to the sky.

Most of the tests lately had been igniter tests. After months of melting engines into slag (a fun activity for a pyromaniac, a nightmarish one for an engineer), and just one centrifuge spin, the propulsion team had decided to revert to the fundamentals. This meant starting back with the most basic component, the igniter, a puny, unglamorous spark—a pilot light, really—which lights a rocket's main engine flame. The term *igniter* comes from the word *ignition,* which means the act of causing a substance or mixture to burn. (This stands in contrast to *explosion,* which means the act of causing an entity to burst apart violently, or blow up.) An igniter is typically lit four to eight seconds before the engine proper, and that interval allows the propellant and oxidizer to mix and thus to emit a smooth tongue of flame. The reason engines have igniters is to prevent explosions in rocket chambers, a phenomenon referred to euphemistically as a *hard start.* A hard start results when an excess of gases accumulates in the rocket chamber and those gases explode, releasing their energy all at once.

On a psychological level, a hard start seemed to be in the works out at the test site. Over the past few weeks, without serious firepower, the crew's potential energy had overaccumulated, and to make matters worse, they were testing silane igniters, silane being a pyrophoric gas, or a gas that combusts when it comes into contact with air. Near dusk one evening, one of the lead test hands started murmuring vagaries, that the test site had been "a real psychological journey," that the place had taught him "some really dark things." That night he started the countdown only from five. The number one was followed by a hiss, a pop, a dim blue flame, and a cynical "whooo hoooo." All the desert had to offer that evening was silane running into an igniter, and the igniter—attached to the test stand, protected from the wind in a Hills Brothers coffee can—a feeble flame. "This is just like kissing your sister," he said. He slammed the door of his truck and drove back out through the airplane graveyard, the small controlled fire bringing no peace, the rockets, for that night at least, fanning rather than burning out life's uneasy, urging flame.

According to *The New Shorter Oxford English Dictionary,* pyromania is "a mania for setting things on fire," mania meaning "a mental disturbance characterized by great excitement or elation, extravagant delusions or over-activity." The American Psychiatric Association's *Diagnostic and Statistical Manual of Mental Disorders, Fourth Edition,* or *DSM-IV,* defines pyromania as an "impulse-control disorder" characterized by "deliberate and purposeful fire setting on more than one occasion" and often accompanied by one or more of the following traits: fascination with, interest in, curiosity about, or attraction to fire and its situational contexts (e.g., paraphernalia, uses, consequences); tension or affective arousal before the act; and pleasure, gratification, or relief when setting fires, or when witnessing or participating in their aftermath. In a perhaps too-interested paper entitled "Pyromania," John Hamling further posits that fire is "peculiarly well-suited for the gratification or sublimation of the male sexual urge." Many of the single men in Mojave tried to address that urge by driving on weekends to Palmdale, or even to Hollywood, in pursuit of dates. But those forays generally met with little success; thus Mojave continued to display a superabundance of fireworks, especially come the Fourth of July, when Christopher drove over to a co-worker's house with a twelve-pack of soda and two buckets full of bomb-making supplies, one of chlorates and the other of sulfates.

Upon his arrival, the entire extended family sat out on the back deck listening to radio dispatches from a fire-fighter relative. Meanwhile Christopher's friend Roger, a Rotary Rocket machinist, tended thirty pounds of tri-tip steak on a fifty-five-gallon-drum grill.

"Hey ya, Short Stack," Christopher yelled.

"Hey yourself," Roger yelled back.

Christopher picked up Roger's three-year-old son and flipped him back onto the ground over his shoulder. He then carried his buckets back to a stiflingly hot workshop where he arranged his mason jars on a crowded bench.

"Look at this stuff," Christopher said, holding up a jar of fine white grains. "I love it. It just looks so ominous." He pulled on safety goggles and big white welding gloves and started making bombs.

To make Smitherite, Christopher Smith's signature flash powder, he mixed fourteen parts potassium chlorate, ten parts aluminum powder, and six parts strontium sulfate, measuring each chemical onto a sheet of white bond paper and funneling the powder into a Foster's Freeze bowl. "A sweatshop," he said. "I love it." The thermometer read 120 degrees. Christopher started singing, "I love Paris in the springtime, I love Paris in the fall, I love Paris in the summer, when it sizzles . . ." He stirred his white concoction with an old screwdriver. It looked like powdered sugar.

Back outside, on the lawn, Christopher poured a teaspoonful onto a leaf of paper, cut a short fuse, and laid it on top.

"What's *that*?" the three-year-old asked.

"That's flash powder."

The boy shrugged and walked away.

The sample worked beautifully, like a lightbulb exploding, so Christopher returned to the shop and funneled his Smitherite into thumb-long lengths of PVC tubing, securing a cap on each end and threading fuses through the holes he'd punctured in the sides. Back outside, he arranged the egg-like cylinders on the wooded deck. "You see this?" Christopher asked the little boy, exposing a white burn scar on the inside of his elbow. "You play with fire, you get burned. You burn down houses. Hahaha."

After dinner, the boy's sister, six years old, pulled out a drawing pad and wrote her name in large block letters. She wrote her brother's as well, and as the neighbors' fireworks began, she drew a house with a chimney, windows, door, flower beds, and a lawn. On top she drew a mess of black squiggles. Ants? Birds? She obliterated her picture.

"What are all those black lines?" an aunt asked, confused.

"Those are fireworks," she said.

The children's father had received two huge boxes of fireworks, free, from the Little League team he'd allowed to set up a fireworks stand at the Foster's Freeze franchise he owned. Now he lit them off in rapid-fire bunches, in between igniting bleach-bottle acetylene bombs. Simultaneously Christopher exploded his homemade stash, his bombs erupting excruciatingly loud and bright, one after the other. The kids wanted him to stop, their aunt wanted him to stop, Roger's wife wanted him to stop, but somehow Christopher couldn't. He blew right through his homemade arsenal and ducked into the workshop to replenish his stores.

"Here I go with my bad self," Christopher said, "bringing a fountain outside." A few minutes later: "Here I go with my bad self carrying barium sulfate."

Finally the kids broke down and joined the madness. "First your turn, then my turn, then your turn, then my turn," the six-year-old instructed her brother until they too exhausted themselves and their father's stores. At around ten, Christopher carried his buckets back out to his truck, preparing to drive to Cal City. "I hate July fifth," he said, dropping me off at White's. "Three hundred and sixty-four more days. I always wake up so depressed."

In late August, Christopher loaded up his truck again, this time with his Solstice rocket and his Rubbermaid prep kits. Earlier he'd helped me pick out a model rocket of my own—flipping through catalogs, asking of each picture, "How does it make you feel?" But by summer's end I still hadn't built my SM-3 Seahawk, I'd just left it in my car. So followed by a short caravan of Rotary employees, I headed with Christopher into the sage scrub and bladder brush for a high-powered rocket launch rally, hoping to understand what fueled his pyromania and to get my own lazy thrills.

On our way we stopped to watch a few minutes of the spectacularly depressing California City Desert Tortoise Day Parade, the meager floats and parched kids lining the too-wide California City Boulevard, and Miss Lancaster, complete in sash and tiara, waving from the back of a Jeep. Christopher parked his truck and ducked into a grocery store to buy some shredded lettuce—batting for his rocket—and when he returned, Miss Lancaster had parked right beside him, so hot and tired and hungry from her waving duties that she'd pulled off the route for Chinese food. Later that morning, driving east toward Roger's Dry Lake, Christopher found a small desert tortoise lying dazed on the tar, its back legs thick and columnar, like a tiny elephant. "Holy crap," he said, pushing it tenderly back onto the sand. He then turned us onto a dusty track and asked if we could talk about girls.

"It makes no sense," he started out, eyes focused on shimmering flats, formerly used by Edwards Air Force Base as a twenty-five-mile-long runway. "I met this girl, on a layover in Atlanta. We got bumped off the same flight." He said he'd liked her immediately, especially her perfume, and shortly after returning to Cal City, he'd written her a poem and sent her a ticket, and she'd come to visit from Louisiana for the weekend. The days passed quickly—movies, giggles, the Black Angus Steakhouse—and a few weeks later she'd agreed to visit again, but this time she canceled just days before her trip. "Now why would a person do that?" he asked, his eyes searching for answers in the circles of creosote clones, in light described by John C. Van Dyke as "so clear at times the truth itself is deceptive." He lifted a hand off the wheel, and smacked his chest. "She just hit me right here."

In the days following the letdown, Christopher had poured himself into making a rocket motor, the result of which now sat between us in his cab: an eighteen-inch-long, two-inch-diameter, stainless steel cylinder, threaded and lathed by hand, and packed with three-quarters of a pound of celadon green propellant. The motor felt strong and balanced, like a fine chef's knife. It had a total impulse of 1,700 Newton-seconds, meaning that if you powdered the propellant grains and ignited them, you could put a car-size hole in the ground.

A few miles off the road, a freestanding metal arch bowed out of the scrub and hardpack. Nearby stood a cinder blockhouse, and fifty yards behind it, crude sand bunkers: narrow ditches covered with telephone poles. Several of the Rotary guys had already arrived, including Ken, the tiny purple sneakers of his young deceased daughter hanging from his rearview mirror. For ninety minutes, we discussed prefab versus spray-on truck bed liners, and ate peanuts and drank water and beer. Finally the launch director, red bandana around his brown neck, called through his bullhorn for us to move under cover for safety.

"Air and road checks, please," he cried, a duty the assembled performed with great solemnity, though who could possibly be on the road or in the air? Most of my fifty bunker mates carried with them binoculars, fast-action cameras, and video cameras. Many carried two. Each launch—a fizz, a pop, a trail of smoke—provided about ten seconds' worth of entertainment. The launches came in sets of three or four. Between them, more peanuts and water and beer.

In the early afternoon, Christopher hauled his three Rubbermaid toolboxes over to the shaded launch prep area and laid his Solstice rocket—black base, blue nose, fluorescent yellow-green cone—atop the wooden bench. Like a surgeon, he worked confidently and with precision, coiling bungee cords, setting timers, installing his stainless steel engine, choosing and folding parachutes, feeling their drag in the blowing air. Just before sealing it up, he packed inside a wad of shredded lettuce and a stuffed animal of a blue-footed booby. A gangly man in a Boeing shirt leaned over from the next prep station.

"You work for Rotary?"

Christopher nodded.

"You're really out there on the jagged edge, aren't you?"

The launch director then bullhorned everyone back into the bunkers, and Christopher, working fast and alone, threaded his rocket onto a long, straight launch rod. The physical locale could not have been less inspiring, but back in the blockhouse Christopher hit the ignition and the Solstice shot up, rising over a mile, 6,500 feet, trailing behind it a soft, mint-green flame. "Man, I'm good!" Christopher shouted, watching his rocket tear through the sky. "I'm *good*!" He ran outside, thumping his chest. He pointed a nearby wheelbarrow in the direction he believed the Solstice would land. "Man, I'm good." He whacked his chest again. "Oooooo, lordy, lordy, this is *fun*!"

For two hours we hiked over the cracked lake bed, through the Parry saltbrush and panamint parsley, five of us fanning out like a search party looking for the Solstice and its fluorescent yellow-green cone. After a couple of miles, hungry and bruised by the stinging nettles, we turned around and Christopher found the rocket in a knot of jumping cholla. "Whooooeeee, this was a big day for Smithereen!" he said when we returned to his truck. He flopped across the blistering front bench. "It doesn't get much better than this! This might be the greatest day of my life!"

11

Two months later, at the end of September, a perfect, clear autumn fell over Silicon Valley and Gary hid inside his Redwood Shores office, the room half-packed with boxes, many bristling with models of failed flying ships. Less than eighteen months from when he claimed he'd have his first Roton in orbit, Gary sat, baggy-eyed and sour-mouthed, elbows slouched against his desk, hands cradling his face. He had lost his sublease from All Bases Covered, the high-tech start-up next door, which would have been a mere annoyance instead of a major calamity had local rents not doubled in the past twenty months, and had Gary not allowed his optimism to get the better of him—had he not allowed his fiscal situation to slip. The only new space he claimed he could find was 18,000 square feet in a leafy office park for $45,000 a month. That, plus his fifty employees and his construction and ATV projects, meant that Rotary Rocket's drip-rate was now approaching two million dollars monthly. Gary waved a draft of a lay-off letter. Had he shown Walt Anderson this? No.

"But I do have a plan," he announced, regaining composure. "We're trying to close our Series C round of financing. We're going out to a broad group for a private placement of $45 million, a group with deep pockets and a proven interest in technology and space." Series A had been the company founders. Series B, friends and family. Who might be approached for Series C?

Gary straight-lined his mouth. "Names like David Geffen, Bill Gates, Paul Allen, Steve Forbes, James Cameron, Tom Hanks, Ross Perot."

Several of the boxes on the floor contained the glossy, tightly printed private placement memos (PPMs), letter-size white brochures, the words $45,000,000 SERIES C CONVERTIBLE PREFERRED STOCK on the front, computer-generated images of the Roton on the back. Gary rolled a slick copy in his hand, forming a shiny baton. "I believe this thing is nearly worthless," he said. "Look at this." He unfurled, flipped, scowled. "There's a nineteen-page spreadsheet in here that was derived from thirty seconds of neurons firing in my head. *How many times can you reuse the engine? How much will the airframe cost?* Making a judgment on this is like building a building on shifting sand. Any investor who believes in these numbers is insane."

Browsing, I noticed that the memo trumpeted the glories of the RocketJet engine (still entirely unbuilt) and the water-transpiration thermal cooling system, which was comprised of many thin layers of mesh (Gary as a joke had tested this by attaching a sample to the front license plate holder of his BMW, but it quickly clogged up with bugs). Gary kept talking: "(a), either investors are going to believe in the Roton concept or they're not going to believe in the Roton concept, and (b), either the Roton concept is going to work, or it's not going to work and nothing in here can make any difference." He looked at me, then flinched his eyes away. "I'm going to put this thing on the table and say, 'This is what the lawyers made me say!' "

Anne, ever attentive, knocked on the door and reminded her husband of an appointment to go screen the latest edit of the Roton video—a crucial tool in the next round of fundraising—so we all drove down Route 101, Gary still ranting, "Look, the Roton could cost $120 million or it could cost $160 million, but when it's all said and done and we've got half the market, what difference does it make?" The day was benign, crystalline, the eucalyptus leaves shuttering like sequins in the wind. "I mean, how do you write a business plan for the DC-3? Or for the transcontinental railroad? It doesn't work to say, 'Here's an idea of the cost and here's an idea of the reward.' You're introducing a technology that's revolutionary, not evolutionary. The degree that you have to rationalize, justify the investment, is different than if you're doing another automotive company or the eighty-fourth disk drive company this year. If an investor doesn't believe in the future potential, no spreadsheet in the world is going to make a difference."

In the passenger seat, Anne looked saintly but drained. She wore a white blouse and white slacks and had dark circles under her eyes. "I was at the printer's twelve hours yesterday," she interrupted her husband, turning around to address me, "and twelve hours the day before, and twelve hours the day before that, but I missed Monday because I was sick with the flu." Anne, sweet woman, fell sick an awful lot. In the past six months, she'd had a systemic yeast infection, three separate sinus infections, uncountable common colds, and many exotic ailments, none of which I can name, because it always seemed too rude to write them down. Now, in a charming rush, she described all the wet and dry snacks at the printer's facility, the free pool and Ping-Pong tables, and the endless war of words between Rotary's bankers and Rotary's lawyers—the former eager to highlight the company's capabilities, the latter insisting on brutal restraint.

Gary placed a hand on his wife's knee. "It's okay, dear, you can calm down now."

"I *am* calm!" Anne insisted. "It's just that we finished at noon, and it's not out of my system yet."

The Fat Box animation studio jutted out over the San Francisco Bay, a blue-shingled split-level with a wrap-around porch, like a classy Cape Cod motel. Upstairs, a young man in long corduroy shorts led us to a screening room, where CFO Rick, sweater tied around his neck, had already installed himself on a couch. Lights dimmed, tape cued up, Fat Box played for us an even more polished version of the Roton animation—pilots' brows furrowed under their helmets, stars visible through the spaceship windows—followed by a ten-minute vanity documentary about the Rotary Rocket company, a sequence that bounced back and forth between black-and-white and color, close-up and long-range shots. Building 31 photographed fantastically, as did the whirl stand, its talon-like tip rockets turning patiently in the wind. Not one of the engineers had worn glasses for the taping. Gary focused down the camera barrel, saying, "For years, I was a lone voice crying in the wilderness."

When the lights came up, Rick started in. "I think you've done an excellent job here, and you should really be very proud of yourselves, but I do have a few concerns. My first is that I wondered if we should see stars out the Roton windows. It's a nice artistic touch, very evocative, but I'm not sure from the angle we're at if you'd actually see them on the way up. Also, I think the *ck-chunk* noise of the landing gear is wrong. I think it should be closer to a *chunk-cshsh*."

Gary slunk lower and buried his head in his chest as Rick questioned the Roton's liftoff and landing—concerns about the shadows. "I think what we have here is an evening-afternoon-evening sequence," Rick concluded after making the filmmaker rewind the tape several times. In his own defense, the filmmaker explained that those images came from actual photographs.

"A nonstarter: we need to fix it," Rick insisted. "The video implies the Roton cannot travel to space and back in a single day."

Upon leaving Gary demanded the new cut by "Wednesday latest," and twenty minutes later he stood back in his office, gazing blankly at the towers of boxes, the models of ocean liners and earthbound rocketships. The phone rang with a jolt. "Hello," Gary answered, startled. "Yes. Hi, Patrick. . . . Yes, I just noticed it in a pile at home. . . . Yes, Anne did call my attention to it. We've had a few problems in accounting. . . . Yes, I know. . . . I'll cut the check next week."

Five days later, money running short, new videos in tow, Gary and Rick flew to New York on an emergency fundraising mission—to meet with venture capitalists as arranged by Barclays, Gary's investment bank. Gary, who had not been to the city in ten years, left a day early to visit his parents in Minnesota. Rick, full of contempt and embarrassed—this was a financial crisis, he was CFO—arrived at the airport a scant six minutes before departure, giddily waving Gary's passport in his small, soft hand.

"Look at this," he said, rosy-cheeked and cocky, "this is the most boring passport in the world." He pulled open the blue flaps, revealing a visa page with only one stamp. Rick had been asked by Gary to pick up the passport just in case Mr. L, the

Canadian man who'd declined to invest in the Rotary ship, changed his mind while Gary was in New York and wanted to invest in the Roton rocket. "What kind of person wants to explore the universe but doesn't want to travel the planet?" Rick scowled. On board, he took a roomy first class seat—he refused to fly coach—next to a man who designed shipping containers. "This guy is really very interested in the Roton concept," Rick reported back on the ground at Kennedy. "It's really a great fit. He promised to watch the video. I always make my best connections up in first class."

The next morning, far downtown, Gary pushed through Barclays' heavy revolving door, entering a lobby adorned with severe modern art, stick figures with big shoulders and small heads that looked ready to roll. He wore a dark, charcoal gray suit and a light gray flannel topcoat, and greeted me by saying, "As Han Solo said, 'I have a bad feeling about this one.' " He dropped his purple duffel at his feet and walked over to the desk to phone up to Richard Smithies, his banker, the one soul he knew in New York. "I'm currently missing a speaking engagement with the Kern County Board of Selectmen," Gary lamented upon his return. He studied his watch—9:10 A.M.—and picked at the hem of his suit jacket. The security guard denied Gary permission to proceed upstairs unchaperoned. "I think this might be my last visit to New York."

From here, Gary planned to fly directly to Los Angeles for the annual convention of the Space Frontier Foundation, where he would surely bump into the Foundation's, and his own, primary benefactor, Walt Anderson—who, incidentally, still had not been told that Rotary was on the brink of insolvency. Rick showed up at Barclays at 9:40 A.M., a full forty minutes late, and as the two waited for their banker they tensely discussed not fundraising strategies but whether to take a car or a cab back to the airport that afternoon. "I think the car might be nicer," Rick offered, "but the cab might be more convenient."

"I've always wanted to take a New York car. Haven't you always wanted to take a car, Rick?"

The plan for the day was for Gary and Rick to strategize with Richard Smithies early in the morning and then meet as a threesome with venture capitalists in the hope of raising funds. At 9:50 A.M. Richard finally showed up, breathless and disheveled, and after escorting us up a couple of dozen floors he abandoned us in a glass-walled conference room, only returning an hour later. "I'm afraid," he announced, with an impish, Catholic schoolboy grin, "that our eleven o'clock meeting's been canceled, which just leaves our three o'clock with Sandler Capital Management." He folded his arms behind his balding red head. "Sandler's is a family-run venture capital outfit. No particular interest in space. Typically doesn't like to make investments under $3 million."

Gary leaned against a wall and slid his back down to the floor. "Okay," he said, knees crouched to his shoulders, "then we'll hit them up for ten."

In preparation Gary and Rick spent the next hours shuttling back and forth between the Barclays cafeteria (where Rick drank hot chocolate and ate jelly Danishes, trying not to spill on his tie) and the fishbowl conference room (where Gary stuck a finger up his nose and stared at nighttime photographs of rockets firing, his skin looking bloodless and pale next to the dark sky and hot flames). No matter the locale, Rick stated, tic-like, "We really need to get in touch with Walt. We need to talk to Walt," but never made the call. Gary's discourse hopped among three distinct planes: Gary berating himself for postponing the board meeting with Walt until he'd secured financing, Gary discussing how the guy who played Mr. Roarke on *Fantasy Island* also played the villain Khan in *Star Trek 2: The Wrath of Khan,* and Gary improvising dialogue for the Barclays employees he could see through the windows in the hallway: "So when was the last time the monkey mated?" "Terminate the experiment; it's clearly failed."

Richard returned shortly after two o'clock with a box of Rotary Rocket mugs, a stack of color brochures, and a copy of the new Roton video. "So what you really need to do," he said, wiggling his ears, "is find some money. It's tough, it's tough. We're really on a knife edge at the moment. We're at the point where if someone has flat-out declined, and we can do no more damage by going back, that seems positive." He opened a leather folder and read down the list of names, pulling air between his teeth. "George Lucas, no. We sent a package to George Lucas. David Geffen, no. Steven Spielberg, no. Craig McCaw, no. Fred Smith, no." This recital felt too cruel, even for Richard, so he switched to naming parties who'd invested instead. "Bob Weinburg. Bob could put in more. Tom Kettleman, I doubt. The Wilcoxes, I kinda don't think so. The Wu family. Alan Chung." Gary blew his nose in his handkerchief. "And Walt Anderson! Walt Anderson we know. And that's the end of the existing!"

On the way up East River Drive toward Sandler Capital Management, Gary began warming up. "We don't need your money! We don't need your money! Screw you and the horse you rode in on!" He rolled down his window and pushed his hands down on the seat, as if he might try to stand. Finally, after a shocking and

minor episode of getting lost, we all climbed onto the raised cement steppe across Fifth Avenue from the Plaza Hotel, Gary's last
and only hope at raising the $45 million he needed to close Series
C. In the elevator, Richard said to Gary, "Anything technical,
that's your baby." To Rick, he said, "Financials, that's your baby
and mine."

Sandler Capital Management occupied one of those beautiful,
home-style offices that makes visitors feel low-class, the kind of
place where you imagine having a nervous breakdown, kicking
and screaming and drooling on the rug, and being hauled off by
security guards who emerge, impeccably groomed, from places
unseen. Rows of small, morbid lucite-encased prospectuses, deal
toys from roadshows, like bugs encased in amber, lined the reception room shelves. Humanely, after only twenty minutes, a secretary shepherded us into one of the principal's suites, and there a
young director in a very short skirt and very large diamonds
graced us with fifteen minutes of her time. Fifteen minutes, full
of interruptions, with peals of laughter bubbling out at the slightest mention of technical detail. "No," the young director assured
Rick, "I have not watched the video, and I don't intend to."

"You'll enjoy it!" Rick pestered. "I guarantee! You'll show it to
your friends!"

Face-out on the desk beamed family photos in silver frames,
everybody in fresh, matching white T-shirts and perfectly faded
jeans. Gary serviceably articulated his vision of space—rockets
like airliners, anywhere-in-the-world package delivery in a single
day—but no more than five minutes after Rick made the singular
move of suggesting the young director might like to vacation in
Mojave, we stood back on the street.

"So how do you think we did?" Rick asked, Gary too waiting

for an answer, Central Park stretching green before us, Bergdorf Goodman twenty yards away. From here, Gary was flying to Los Angeles, where he'd surely face questions from Walt. Richard raised a hand and hailed a cab. Gary stooped inside, grumbling, upset that no one had arranged for a car.

12

Gary's prime benefactor, Walt Anderson, was a man with white hair, pale skin, square, gold-rimmed glasses, and a physical presence so profoundly unprepossessing it was almost impossible to remember what he looked like. He was forty-five—a product, like Gary, of the *You Among the Stars, You and Space Neighbors, You Will Go to the Moon* generation—and he'd once considered commissioning a painting for his apartment based on the Smashing Pumpkins' pop lyric "Rat in a Cage." "That's what we are," Walt told me the first time I met him, "rats in a cage. And we're going to gnaw through the bars because we've got about a thirty-year window here and we'll starve if we don't get out."

The cage Walt referred to was the planet Earth itself, and he'd taken it upon his shoulders to ensure that we get off. He'd grown up in Silver Spring, Maryland, in a community of Holocaust survivors. Though his parents were not among them, this dark history forged both his misanthropy and his philanthropy. He'd discovered early on an innate facility for making money and an unprecedented willingness to spend that money on traveling into space. In 1972, at age eighteen, he began hiring out his friends to wash windows and clean carpets for ten dollars an hour and charging his clients twenty-five. Seven years later, in 1979, he became one of the first 300 employees at MCI, and in 1984, he founded MidAtlantic Telecom, a "small, regional" long-distance carrier, the first to integrate phone and voicemail service. Seven years after that, in 1991, he started Esprit Telecom, cracking into the newly deregulated European market. In 1993 he became the fund manager of the British Virgin Islands holding company Gold & Appel, named after *The Golden Apple,* the second volume in the 1970s sex-and-conspiracy-theory cult pulp novels *The Illuminatus! Trilogy.* The company was seeded with $6.2 million, and Walt had been in the habit of more or less doubling its capital every year since. In 1998, George Soros's Global TeleSystems bought Esprit Telecom for $985 million in stock and assumed debt. A chunk of that money would go on to be used to build rockets and fund space companies.

Did this not make NASA extremely nervous?

"In my life," Walt said, "if the U.S. government doesn't try to kill me, I probably won't have succeeded in meeting my long-term goals."

Walt now lived in Washington, D.C., a city he claimed to hate, resulting, one imagined, from the fact that his father had worked as a Cold Warrior for the top-secret National Security Agency, and he had not spoken to his father in twenty-five years. (Walt refused to answer questions about his childhood or his psyche.) Over dinner one night in a French eatery in Georgetown, he told me he'd drink champagne if Henry Kissinger were convicted of war crimes. If a volunteer were needed for the execution, he said he'd gladly pull the trigger. He made incendiary remarks about all kinds of world leaders—Clinton, Netanyahu—and he professed an inability to understand how a government could manufacture weapons of mass destruction and still care about the advancement of the human race. He also boasted, nonchalantly, that he was trying to save *Mir* and rent it. But at the time I failed to take him seriously, never imagining his biggest clash with Uncle Sam would occur over a third-generation Soviet-era space station designed to orbit only five years, but already spinning almost a decade beyond its expected life.

During its fourteen years, *Mir* garnered many nicknames—the porcupine, the dragonfly—most referring to its ungainly assortment of modules and solar arrays. Its exterior resembled six school buses gridlocked at an intersection, yellowed and pocked with propellant stains. Inside it remained just as aesthetically unpleasing, clogged with cables, crammed with gear, smelling like sweaty feet. The first module, the base block, had been sent into orbit in February 1986. But by the end of the eighties, the Soviet empire collapsing, the station was beset by significant money worries. As early as 1992, top Russian space officials were comparing their peripatetic program to a chicken: "You cut off its head and it runs around the yard for a while thinking it's still alive."

NASA too dragged and sputtered during that same period. From the *Challenger* accident, in January 1986, until September 1988, the agency remained grounded, and while its return to space was nominally triumphant (the shuttle seemed to work fine), in reality it mostly proved to the country that NASA had no clear mission. President George H. W. Bush tried to help the situation in 1989 by declaring, John F. Kennedy–style, that an American would walk on Mars within thirty years. In 1992 he tried again, hoping to gain points in the polls against Bill Clinton, this time declaring that a space shuttle would dock at the Russian station *Mir* and the two ships would swap crew members, symbolizing the end of the Cold War. He still lost the election, and suffice it to say even the Russian cosmonauts were not impressed. The deal was six days on the unsafe shuttle in exchange for three months on the ultrasafe *Mir*? It hardly sounded fair. Yet after enough political pressure from Washington and Moscow—and a compromise involving NASA paying Russia $400 million—in March 1995 the astronaut Norman Thagard became the first United States citizen to live aboard *Mir*. Shannon Lucid followed one year later, staying from March to September 1996, and breaking the American record for time spent in space.

In 1997 *Mir* suffered a string of high-profile, high-altitude disasters—a collision, a fire, and several massive computer shutdowns. The goodwill program limped along as scheduled for at least another year, but by August 1999, *Mir*'s troubles had grown so vast and so economically intimidating that the Russians decided to abandon their outpost and call their final crew in. NASA, carefully tracking Russia's limited resources—the Russians were, by that point, more than a year late on launching the service module, or living quarters, for the International Space Station—waxed ecstatic. That is, until October 1999, when in a move that the chairman of the House Science Committee would call "a real kick in the jaw," Walt Anderson flew to Moscow to meet with Yuri Semenov, general-director of the private Russian space corporation Energia, playing the board game Risk along the way. Upon arrival, one of the first things Walt said to Semenov was, "I don't necessarily agree with the views of my government."

Within three days he'd made a verbal agreement to lease the space station *Mir*.

It was not just an act of civil defiance. In most ways it was an act of devotion, trust, and faith. Walt had been dreaming of leaving Earth since he was a little boy. On behalf of a new company he'd founded called MirCorp, he'd wired the Russians $7 million before he even signed *Mir*'s lease. That lease, which MirCorp seeded with $21 million against an eventual $200 million, would later give MirCorp the rights to *Mir* for the remainder of its lifetime, the use of two or three manned Soyuz rockets and two or three unmanned Progress rockets, the exclusive control of *Mir*'s visitors and technologies, forty days of active operation, and the privilege of fixing *Mir* up. For an additional $10 million, MirCorp would further gain another Soyuz rocket and two cosmonauts to ride in it. And perhaps most important to Walt's anti-government sensibility, MirCorp would insinuate itself financially into bed with Energia, much to the dismay of NASA, the agency then in trouble, as it had been for ten years, with the way-over-schedule, way-over-budget, politically Pollyanna-ish International Space Station.

That station, ISS, originally named space station *Freedom*, had been announced in 1983 under President Ronald Reagan, and had already suffered the embarrassment of two congressional investigations, though the most zealous space patriots in Washington still clamored for it to be "the only space in space." The vision was grand. The materials necessary to build the station in space required forty-three rocket launches. A collaborative effort of sixteen countries, ISS would eventually support a full-time crew of seven, the astronauts working together in a 460-ton, 46,000-cubic-foot suite, roughly the size of two 747 jets. The reality of ISS, however, was to prove less compelling. In 1998, nonplussed with NASA's ceaseless wheel-spinning and cost overruns, Newt Gingrich credited ISS with making "space as boring as possible" and *The Economist* magazine dubbed the behemoth "the black hole in the sky." (By 1999, ISS was projected to cost the United States $17.4 billion, more than twice the $8 billion originally planned. At this writing, the cost to the United States had risen to $28.2 billion and problems with the international coalition were growing worse.) Still, a less brusque man than Walt might have chosen to sweet-talk and mollify the NASA brass. But he was arrogant in such matters, "an anarcho-capitalist" as he called himself, flying around the world in a private jet pledging allegiance to the laws of GATT. So instead of calling NASA about *Mir,* Walt called instead his friend Chirinjeev "Baboo" Kathuria, a thirty-five-year-old mega-millionaire Sikh. In response, Baboo told Walt he too was "interested" in *Mir,* which in mega-millionaire-speak meant he was willing to chip in $5 million and start upsetting the last century's notions of international relations in space.

At the tail end of March 2000, Walt invited me to join him in Amsterdam, just a few days before he was to launch the world's inaugural privately funded manned mission into space, and less than a week before the two cosmonauts he had hired would enter *Mir* to see if it could be repaired. At that time, his plans for *Mir* included rehabbing the station and expanding its volume to nine or ten times its present size. He had structured MirCorp—based in the Bahamas, run out of Amsterdam—as a forty-sixty partnership with Energia, 38 percent of which is owned by the Russian government. His space talk was still infused with statements that sounded vaguely like clubhouse rules. ("I'm not saying it's fair, but I've been thinking a lot about human rights in space, and in my space station, people would all be peaceful or I'd throw them out the airlock.") He intended to sell joyrides to *Mir* to wealthy individuals (Dennis Tito, the money manager and former rocket engineer who would eventually fly to ISS, originally signed on with Walt as the first space tourist); advertising on *Mir* to commercial companies ("we'll paint it up like a NASCAR"); access to equipment to various world governments; and later to move into novel, dubious, and potentially extremely lucrative markets, such as in-orbit satellite assembly and satellite repair. He also harbored a taste for high-skies vigilantism. As he said in the American Hotel's dully plush lobby, "If I discover dirty satellites, nuclear weapons in orbit, am I going to pretend they're not there? No."

Walt's partner Baboo turned up in Amsterdam the next day in a bright red turban and met me for a cheeseburger lunch. Baboo had just flown in from Chicago, where he had been living with his parents, sleeping in the same bed he'd slept in as a teenage boy. His eyes were so wide they were almost round. His long beard was tacked to his chin with bobby pins. "*Mir* is definitely a real business," he said, starting to giggle, his voice growing high and airy and soft, "definitely undervalued" and "definitely cool." By Baboo's estimation, *Mir* was much cooler than the telecom business, through which he'd met Walt. Baboo had fallen into that business when he developed a crush on the heiress to a Filipino telecom fortune, and tried to impress her by, along with his family, privatizing India's phones.

After lunch, in the brief window before Baboo was to meet Walt for a second cheeseburger at Burger King, where the two would commit to invest another $10 million in *Mir,* we walked along the canals to the Van Gogh museum to stand among the masses staring at sad, starry skies. Along the way, Baboo remembered the time he sat in a limo outside the Miss Universe Contest in Trinidad with Donald Trump, who was making out with a twenty-three-year-old girl, and Evander Holyfield, who'd wanted to borrow his "hat." In the morning he would be flying to Moscow with MirCorp president Jeffrey Manber to watch Mir-Corp's first launch. (Walt was not coming. He was flying instead from Amsterdam to Spain, then to France.) If all went according to plan, if the launch succeeded and the docking succeeded, Mir-Corp would be the first private company to send civilians to space. If the launch failed or the docking failed, MirCorp would be responsible for the deaths of two Russian cosmonauts, inciting an international catastrophe.

Moscow, when we reached it, was gray and in a state of flux, with the new IKEA out by the airport and the new mall under the Kremlin, a warm streak turning the vast countryside to mud, and daily articles in the papers about what kind of leader Putin would be. According to the Russian philosopher Grigori Pomerants, his country had slipped into "a state of mass disorientation" since the collapse of the Soviet empire. MirCorp's presence here surely did not help. It came with its fat wallets, its precocious grand masters of capitalism, buying at deep discount the detritus of the space race, the Soviet Union, the Cold War.

On the surface, the situation sounded like the setup for a joke: *So there's a Sikh and an anarcho-capitalist and they want to buy a space station. . . .* Beneath it, the reality was more desperate and more gonzo. From Moscow, Baboo, Jeffrey, and I drove to the soot-covered industrial suburb of Korolev, where, via monitors at Energia, we watched the successful launch of the cosmonaut-carrying Soyuz rocket. Baboo then spent the next forty-eight hours muttering repeatedly, "This is definitely not telecom, definitely not for the faint of heart," all the while sitting in meeting rooms in Energia's international building—a square, pale, brick box at the end of a pitted cul-de-sac, with no front door, no lobby, no ornamentation, an international building only possible to design if the architect never imagined foreign guests. Not long ago these austere, heatless rooms had housed debates about missile capability and Iron Curtain strategy so geopolitically intense and affecting that they sent schoolchildren across America scurrying under their desks for bomb drills. Now agenda items included wiring *Mir* as an Internet portal; co-producing a television show with *Survivor* producer Mark Burnett entitled *Who Wants to Go to Space?* (later billed as *Destination: Mir*, later scrubbed); and patenting all possible technologies onboard the station, thereby precluding NASA, or so Walt hoped, from "building so much as an airlock without paying MirCorp something first."

How did this happen? Only due to an odd amalgam of hubris, politics, cash, and timing did *Mir* wind up in private hands. Russia, turmoil-ridden and economically desperate, hated to lose its most visible symbol of Soviet technical prowess, and Walt, riding the crest of the biggest financial high in history, salved the faltering nation's pride, his ego, and his childhood obsession with space travel by buying in. Doing so, he cast himself as the big-hearted border-hopping savior of the station in distress. As a result, the Russians sounded swoony and charmed by their MirCorp deal ("Investment not so fair from [MirCorp's] part," a chief Energia officer gloated to me), while NASA chief Dan Goldin sounded defensive, embarrassed, and left out.

"My feelings are bruised," said Goldin, sounding like a sidelined mafioso, when I reached him in his office in D.C. "I have a hurt. I'm not saying they shouldn't have done what they did, I'm just saying I'm in the book, they've got my number, and it might have been nice if they called."

Goldin sounded conflicted and disrespected for good reason. Conflicted because, theoretically at least, the NASA administrator favored space commercialization. "Competition is great!" rang one of his mantras. Under his watch, NASA had awarded $3 billion annually in contracts to fledgling space businesses (Walt refused to accept such funds on the Roton project, and he refused to accept them for *Mir*), and even yoked together Boeing and Lockheed Martin in an effort to privatize the space shuttle fleet. But at the same time, unseemingly, his bureaucracy had hemorrhaged billions on ISS.

In 1999 NASA had suffered one of its worst years ever, losing two robotic landers on Mars. So while he was sincere in saying, "If this MirCorp can finance *Mir* and get a positive cash flow, an unsubsidized positive cash flow, I think that's fabulous!" he was just as humiliated to have to explain to Congress why (a) the Russians were failing to meet their ISS milestones while simultaneously saving *Mir,* and (b) a certain international financier was able to negotiate far better prices than he was.

"I'm not saying that money is being diverted," Goldin protested, intimating that the Russians may have been siphoning money from ISS and dumping it into *Mir.* "I'm just saying the arithmetic doesn't add up. I read in the papers that private United States investors paid $20 million, and for $20 million they get, I don't know, six weeks of operation of the *Mir* space station, a Soyuz vehicle, a Progress vehicle. They got the operations center. They got the training. And now I understand they're going to get *another* flight up there? The Russians charged us, last year,

$65 million for one Soyuz vehicle! And $135 million for two! I'm just saying that it's just frustrating, year after year, to have to go through the perils of Pauline when the Russian government doesn't fund their own space agency, doesn't give us any vehicles to work with. So like I said, I have some bruised feelings. And the arithmetic! I'm confused."

In Korolev, the morning of the docking, television crews trailed muddy tracks as they pushed through the command and control center's drab marble foyer. The Russian spring is said to resemble an old whore disrobing. The world had gone slack and runny, everyone was in a hurry—who were these rich investors?—and no one was wiping his feet. Upstairs, the control room proper resembled an aging 1950s college lecture hall: dark rows of concentric half-circles, a projection screen up front. Old men filled the back seats, clasping hands and taking pictures, the engineers and cosmonauts of years past: Boris Chertok, eighty-eight years old, who'd commanded the first space docking ever; a still young and mustached Sergei Krikalev, who in 1991 had called down from *Mir* while the Soviet Union disassembled below, asking, "Is it true that Russia is going to sell the *Mir* space station, where we are now? And, we are asking, together with us?" All had seen communism, perestroika, and failed capitalism; all regarded Walt's impertinent largesse with blank, irresolute stares. The only confrontational faces belonged to the American media. Covering the story, a haughty, coiffed NBC commentator stood just above the control room floor taping an aggressive stand-up. "Massaging Russian national pride but aggravating Russian-American relations, international investors have launched two men to the *Mir* space station, causing a situation as rickety as *Mir* itself." The commentator thrust a foam-tipped mike in MirCorp president Jeffrey Manber's face.

NBC: Are you going to compete with the International Space Station?

MirCorp: We believe in a gas station on every corner. We believe in more than one home in space.

NBC: Don't you believe as an American that you're delaying ISS?

MirCorp: I was in the White House when President Ronald Reagan announced the International Space Station *Freedom* seventeen years ago. I believe seventeen years is long enough to wait.

Nearly two hundred miles above, two men careering at 18,000 miles per hour were trying to catch a decrepit space station doing the same. On-screen, the spinning earth was captured under the crosshairs of the docking portal. The image looked haunting—it spoke of power—and one had to wonder what Walt was doing right that moment. Presumably he was making money on phones in France. Or perhaps he was in Spain, pursuing another of his idealistic far-out ventures, like the thermo-protected, rocket-powered, sky-diving space suits a friend of his was trying to build. It was nearly impossible to say—logistically, because nobody had a cell phone number that worked for Walt in Europe, and emotionally, because, like many men of his generation, Walt's cleft personality was hard to resolve. The devil in

Walt, one suspected, was trying to screw his father's government, yet his space-faring impulse seemed to come from a pure, even child-like, place.

Fortunately, the docking itself provided only minor excitement—a bounce off the portal, a switch from automatic to manual before the cosmonauts locked in. But directly afterward, Energia's general-director Yuri Semenov performed one of the boldest, baldest gestures in the history of human space flight. Before the old-timers and gawking reporters, he publicly handed to MirCorp *Mir*'s reins. Everyone laughed aloud with Semenov at the timeless human tragicomedy: the indignities of age, the perpetually rising young. Not heard, however, were the inward nervous twitters, for this was a transition not simply from one generation to the next, or from one political philosophy to another, but from a world order based on governments to one based on wealth, from an old-school Soviet comrade to an anarchic super-citizen; a man who, because of a certain facility for money, had the power to affect relations on a geopolitical scale.

The effects of such a world order, if it in fact comes to pass, will not be known for quite some time. Throughout the year 2000, MirCorp steadily lobbied the Russian government just to keep the beast aloft. Meanwhile, NASA, on the sidelines, continued feeling "bruised" and "hurt," continued its public kvetching and high-pitched tormented gossip, continued exerting pressure on the new president Putin to dump his old space bag into the sea. In the end, NASA got its wish. MirCorp never attracted further investors, and on March 23, 2001, *Mir* crashed down at 900 miles per hour into the southern Pacific Ocean, eluding the jet chartered by some rich Americans to glimpse its fiery demise. Still, for over a year, Walt and Semenov appeared to have jilted

Uncle Sam, and only minutes after the docking, Baboo, as Walt's proxy, found himself enveloped in a pack of elder Energia statesmen and, to consummate their union privately, shepherded into the control room built for ISS. There, among never-used consoles and plastic-wrapped chairs, everyone ate smoked salmon and caviar and drained shots of Standard vodka. Everyone watched as MirCorp's cosmonauts floated through *Mir's* hatch, unfurled the blue-and-white MirCorp sign, and thanked Mir-Corp very much. Semenov toasted his new sugar daddies—"The people who trusted us"—and rebuffed his old flame, NASA—"You closed the door on us. You closed the door in our face." Walt's absence felt enigmatic, awkward. He left no word for almost a week. And when he did, he offered only a single, simple phrase to describe how he felt about forging his new space liaison, how he felt about sending two cosmonauts to orbit, challenging Russian-American relations, and perhaps challenging relations between governments and their wealthiest citizens for quite some time. That phrase illuminated nothing of his personal and political motives. He said plainly, as mercurially as ever, "I'm happy."

13

As soon as Gary arrived at the Space Frontier Foundation conference in Los Angeles he began to feel better. He'd escaped New York, that bastion of doubt, and looked forward to a weekend in the LAX Sheraton, immersed in the subculture that had produced *Kings of the High Frontier,* a science fiction novel starring Gary thinly disguised as the dashing inventor of the Starblazer, a rocket remarkably similar to the Roton and terrifying to NASA because it would work.

The event attracted a larger and wider-ranging crowd than Space Access in Scottsdale, Arizona. Buzz Aldrin and Pete Conrad, both of whom had founded rocket companies of their own, turned out, and at the opening night cocktail party, the Rotary contingent, ten or twelve strong, pranced in a duck-line behind an engineer hoisting overhead a bell-nozzled engine. Gary stood on the sidelines, detached—he knew the engine's curved bell was entirely fake—sipping a glass of Merlot. "I didn't bring my short sword," he mumbled, "so that's good."

Anne stood beside him in a flowing black crepe tunic. "The long sword," she explained, "is for disemboweling the enemy. The short sword is for disemboweling yourself." She then whispered, between us girls, "When the going gets tough, the tough keep a little Xanax in the bottom drawer."

Until Walt's arrival the following day, Gary bided his time with Mike Kelly and Mitch Clapp, and attended symposia on asteroid mining, the Hollywood-spacer connection, and Robert Zubrin's new Mars Society, the manifesto of which proclaimed, "The time has come for humanity to journey to Mars!" I bought a self-published book on lunar habitation and met a man with Coke-bottle glasses and a gap in his mustache, where he habitually placed a finger, who told me, "In a sense I feel like my mind is a microcosm of what happened in the space movement. If you don't dream, you can't live. But if you don't realize the practicalities, you can't live either. The space movement didn't realize the practicalities for many years. It hung a lot of people out to dry. It turned out to just be a special thing for the Cold War."

An impatient, boyish frenzy permeated nearly all conversations, a driving need to believe in something grand, romantic, and beyond. Still, the primary idiom of this conference remained deeply fatalistic, the metaphor of upstart rocket companies (like Rotary Rocket or Pioneer Rocketplane) as being like fledgling mammals banging on the feet of the dinosaurs (the overlarge, inefficient NASA, Lockheed Martin, and Boeing). The image popped up everywhere, in lectures, even on T-shirts. Rightly, it implied that at this point in time, the upstart rocket companies were merely bothersome to the dinosaurs, if noticed at all. Delusionally, it suggested that a meteor would soon hit, causing the monoliths to flounder, after which point the upstarts would thrive no matter what.

Walt stepped out of the elevator the next afternoon wearing black jeans, a suede sport coat, and moccasin-like slippers. (The shoes enabled him to pad soundlessly around the hospitality suite, ghoulishly tying balloons to spacers' wives' hair.) His blanched coloring and slight body called to mind the meddlesome benefactor in *Contact*. By evening, Gary had not yet delivered the financial news, though it hardly mattered. "I like Gary because Gary has failed so many times before," Walt said, having skipped out of the keynote banquet speech. "He's desperate. He's on the edge of disaster but not yet quite over the cliff. The average venture capitalist would laugh Gary out of the room. But I don't have to convince Joe Six Pack. I run a business that's very profitable."

Walt heroized Martin Luther King and Genghis Khan—"for his time, he was very progressive"—and referred to investment bankers as "feral dogs." "It's a challenge, an enormous challenge, to try to start human settlement off-earth. But all creatures need the right amount of challenge or else they die. Even frogs need the right amount of challenge. I know I can build a successful business, and I know I can build a house on a hill, but I don't know if I can do this." The banquet room doors opened and Gary appeared; Walt excused himself, preparing to slip away. "It's the only reason why I'm still working eighty hours a week—I want to change the world, to really change the world. Because while it's certainly nice to read to old people, I'd rather save the next hundred generations from living in their own shit."

Gary's huge new 18,000-square-foot office lay just down the road from a dirt and rock recycling center, and the place was big, far too big for the diminished state of Rotary's ego—with still no word from Walt, Gary couldn't command the space. The front door opened onto a gulping expanse, off which extended two unfinished side suites, each the size of a large suburban house.

Gary's staff had struggled hard to make the place look promising, but the fresh paint on the walls looked too blue, and the bouquet on the reception desk, full of spiky birds-of-paradise, too flamboyant, desperate, and strange. Anne held a vigil by the telephone switchboard, awaiting calls from Series C investors who never rang. Only the office manager appeared content, her wide pear hips snug in her new desk chair. "You haven't seen these drawings yet?" she asked, unrolling the large schematics and blueprints, plans for the living room–style reception lounge, the gym, the shower and bath suite. "The space is just going to be fabulous. Can't you see it? The coffee bar is going to be right over there." She pointed to a Sheetrock wall striped with mud. "That's what I'm most excited about."

A carpenter knelt down to install a new lock on Gary's office door—whether for Gary to lock himself in or to facilitate the day when he'd be locked out, no one could say. Gary himself shrank behind an enormous horseshoe-shaped desk, a box of signed and numbered PPMs by his feet, a Rotary clock, with an orbiting Roton, ticking on the wall. "Barclays sent out all six hundred packets and received four or five maybes in response." He spoke with his hands covering his mouth, making him difficult to understand. "Actually, I think it was six or seven." The numbers kept creeping up, and within an hour, Gary said, Barclays had twenty interested parties, and figuring five or six of those would invest about $5 million each, everything would work out fine, though Gary did admit it'd be "a near-run thing."

"You have to be thinking clearly in a situation like this. You have to be feeling ready to storm the beach." Gary broke into a deep, stately tone, as if imagining himself to be Winston Churchill. "We shall never ever surrender. This particular ship of state, once it's moving at thirteen knots, it's very hard to change course quickly or make it slow down. It takes about twenty days. It's already too late. It's like that moment in the movie when the guy says, 'Bang, you're dead,' and you are, and that's really the worst part. You see yourself dying in such horrific detail, much worse than a director could ever do."

A photograph of Gary in a white Rotary Rocket T-shirt, standing inside the dark, womb-like LOX tank in the Scaled Composites clean room, lay faceup on the desk. He picked it up in a quivering hand, flipped it over, and, for the first time in my presence, started to cry. "We're not a garage operation anymore. Payroll is half a million a month. Scaled is spending about that too. We need three to five million to see us through to the end of the year. That's not a trivial amount of money, but it's a trivial amount of money for building a spaceship, for Christ's sake."

In the vast horseshoe, Gary looked diminutive and exposed, like the unveiled Wizard of Oz. Marti the pilot, already changed into his Rollerblading outfit, poked his head through the door at two o'clock, and Gary said, "There's nothing else for anybody to do here. You should just go home."

The minutes passed painfully. I felt Gary to be at least partially liable for his own failure, and I felt myself to be culpable and silly for being so saddened by his demise. We stared at each other, stuck uncomfortably in the present. Then Gary's phone rang. "Yeah, the damn thing never rings in my office," he said into the mouthpiece, motioning for me to wait outside. "It's a real nuisance . . . Right . . . right . . . right. . . . That seems like a fair price."

A moment later, he stepped out into the hallway, where he

stood expressionless, almost paralyzed, until Anne ran over and his face cracked open with fear, joy, and relief. Walt had allowed Gary to come under the heel of disaster, right to the brink of the cliff. Then he called to say, as if on a whim, that Gold & Appel would like to invest an additional 10 million bucks.

PART
TWO

1

Ten million dollars presented an interesting problem. Ten million dollars was not enough to complete the Roton project; it was only enough to do one thing, and the one thing Gary chose to do was build his glorious, symbolic ATV and roll it out before the press and space world for the purpose of attracting investors. Months beforehand, the media had caught on to the story, profiling Gary and Rotary with amused derision: "Earth to Gary" *(Forbes)*, "Spacecraft Engineers Propose the Mother of All Autorotations" *(Aviation International News)*, "Rotary Rocket Masters of Spin" *(Aviation Week's Space Business)*, "Is Rotary Rocket for Real?" *(Aviation Week's Space Business)*, "On a Rotor-Blade and a Prayer" *(The Economist)*, "It's a Rocket? It's a Chopper? It's Both" *(Business Week)*, "It's a Windmill? It's a Helicopter? No, it's a Rocket!" *(The Asahi Shimbun)*, "And Now For Something Completely Different" *(The Boston Globe)*, and "Going for a Spin" *(The New Scientist)*. Still Gary stuck to his plan to throw his rocket a debutante party. His rollout invitations reflected his wishful attitude—elegant, bright blue with a white Roton drawing, inscribed with the words *If we build it, they will come.*

Leading up to the rollout, Gary hemorrhaged massive quantities of cash, not only on completing his ATV and his massive high/low bay complex, but on extravagant party favors: custom-embroidered Roton bags, custom Roton pens, and custom Roton vanity chocolates, milk, white, and dark. At the same time, not much about the Roton was going well, at least not in the Rotary shop. Gary's propulsion team had produced a functional cooled throat, but many of the other parts of the engine had failed, and someone left one of the valves unpurged, which resulted in silane, a gas that combusts with air, leaking all over the test site shed. Also, inconveniently, Gary had miscalculated the completion date of his low bay, and thus failed to renew his Building 31 lease. The engineers now occupied the bleak and expensive Building 1, the former officers' quarters, a warren of cubbies that lacked all the loft-like pizzazz of Building 31's unfinished space.

"Every engineer has periods where you feel like you can't do a damn thing right," Jeff Greason, the manager of the propulsion team, explained from his office, the eggshell walls badly in need of a fresh coat of paint. "The centrifuge isn't working. I'm worried about the buoyancy effects of spinning an engine. I'm not confident we can find a base thermal protection system that's robust, reusable, and light—that hasn't been engineered at all." He shook a beefy hand, one finger extended for each problem. "I also don't think the guys at the test site have a feel for what they're doing. With the test site I have the feeling the problems won't be solved."

Mojave itself helped matters not at all, despite the best attempts of Roger White, the proprietor of White's Motel. Roger bided his time in his motel lobby flipping his cards and petting his poodles, a pair of thick plastic glasses in each of his two shirt pockets, a voice long wrecked from overuse and cigarettes. "Well, hello there! How are you today!" he called out hopefully to all Rotary affiliates, in fact, to all passersby. On his paneling he'd nailed two deer heads, a stuffed mountain lion, several decades' worth of Mojave Mustang wrestling plaques, and a picture of a childhood friend shaking Bill Clinton's hand.

Roger told stories that focused, by and large, on a single theme: his brushes with great moments in history. He told one about the time Mary Pickford drove him to a football game in Lancaster, another about how he drove through Nebraska at the end of the Dust Bowl, the wind and rain dropping the telephone poles at precisely the same speed as his car. He'd hunted jackrabbits with Chuck Yeager, purchased for $5 Mojave's first Model T, suggested that Roger's Dry Lake be used for testing planes (this resulted, or so he said, in Edwards Air Force Base), and once grown a crop of alfalfa so sweet he'd wrecked the FDA's categories. Sometimes Roger's son Bill sat down, usually in his Mojave Mustangs football sweatshirt. Together the two indulged in one of Roger's favorite pastimes: listing who, over the years, had stayed at White's.

"Raquel Welch, Raquel Welch stayed here."

"Burl Ives!"

"John Wayne!"

"Bob Hope. Bob Hope stayed here. He wore white shorts and a pink polka-dotted shirt."

"Jane Russell."

"Wyatt Earp."

"Lassie had two rooms!"

"Did Dean Martin stay with us?"

"Frank Sinatra!"

"Charlton Heston!"

"Did Cary Grant stay with us?"

"William Boyd."

"What about Errol Flynn? Gable?"

"Bing Crosby used to stop by a lot, but he was always on his way to L.A."

On quieter days, Roger would shuffle to the check-in counter and shuffle back with a black-and-white photo of himself at age seven, sitting on a mule. The Roger in the photo, like the Roger in the office, wore shorts and short ankle socks and a short-sleeve, button-down shirt. But the Roger in the office had legs like waxed paper, and his eyebrows looked like fiberglass, woolly and rough. One evening I joined the extended White clan as they watched Robbie Knievel, Evel's son, jump across the Grand Canyon on a motorcycle without a parachute. On the television, amid the hunting trophies, the couches covered with quilts, Knievel revved back and forth on his wooden ramp while his daughter sang the national anthem in her brave, quavering voice. Unnerved, I asked Roger's daughter Cheryl how she thought a man might train for such a stunt. "You can't," she said, not looking up from her crocheting. "All you can do is prepare to die, and so you pray."

In *The Varieties of Religious Experience,* the definitive text on the subject, the turn-of-the-century psychologist William James defines prayer as "that general name for that attitude of open and earnest expectancy," adding, "If we then ask to *whom* to pray, the answer (strangely enough) must be that *that* does not much matter." Religion James defines broadly, without reference to institution, as "the feelings, acts, and experiences of individual men in their solitude, so far as they apprehend themselves to stand in relation to whatever they may consider divine." The main feature of the religious temperament he describes as the ability to see things differently—in particular, the ability to see dark patches in life as tests, occasions for rejoicing. The inability to do so he describes as the lack of faith.

James also sketches, in his charming, writerly manner—the book was originally a series of lectures delivered at Harvard—the character traits of those most susceptible to religion and religious belief.

> In the psychopathic temperament we have the emotionality which is the *sine qua non* of moral perception; we have the intensity and the tendency to emphasis which are the essence of practical moral vigor; and we have the love of metaphysics and mysticism which carry one's interests beyond the surface of the sensible world. What, then, is more natural than that this temperament should introduce one to regions of religious truth, to corners of the universe, which your robust Philistine type of nervous system, forever offering its biceps to be felt, thumping its breasts, and thanking Heaven that it hasn't a single morbid fiber in its composition, would be sure to hide forever from its self-satisfied possessors?
>
> If there were such a thing as inspiration from a higher realm, it might well be that the neurotic temperament would furnish the chief condition of the requisite receptivity.

While the connection between space culture and religion is obvious, it first became explicit to me six months earlier when, on the day of Gary's high bay groundbreaking, Rotary's data systems manager remarked sotto voce, "These people don't realize it but they're building cathedrals." Rand Simberg was a contractor in his forties, with dark hair, a noodly body, and a car largely missing a dashboard. Shortly thereafter he handed me a Xeroxed copy of a paper he'd written in college, a thesis for an anthropology class exploring the question (chosen by Rand), "What aspects, if any, of the space movement can be considered religious, and are there enough of them to warrant calling the space movement a religious movement?"

In response, Rand had written, "I think, first of all, that if we consider a blind faith in technology to be a form of religion, spacers are demonstrably some of the most religious people on the face of this planet, or any other." Further, "Of more than passing interest is the ultimate goal that spacers are trying to attain. They are very literally going to heaven. On the axis of a spinning colony, there would be zero gravity and a colonist could float blissfully in the clouds, just like we're taught in Sunday school. . . . It is the promised land for techno-freaks. Not only can you go to heaven before you die, you don't even have to die. Many spacers believe that space technology will hold the key to rejuvenation and regeneration. Space, therefore, also offers the ultimate goal that most religions have been striving for for centuries: immortality."

Rand described the space movement as "a culture in exile," a culture "formed in anticipation of a future homeland," just like the early-twentieth-century Mormons and the late-nineteenth-century Zionist Jews. Along with a group of friends he'd met through OASIS, the Organization for the Advancement of Space Industrialization and Settlement, he'd also written a space seder. The seder was heavily derivative in form of the Jewish Passover seder. It commemorated *Apollo 11,* that modern-day exodus, and was told as if to a child living on a space station in the year 2050.

On July 20, I arrived at the home of Rand's friend Bill Simon (or actually, Bill Simon's parents), in Beverly Hills. The Simons lived in a comfortable blue bungalow decorated with the bright impressionistic paintings of Bill's mother, Elsa. Typical of most holidays, by mid-afternoon the kitchen was already in pre-holiday chaos, with Bill's girlfriend decorating the infinity cake (baked in the shape of the symbol ∞, to invoke the infinity of possible new homes in the universe); Bill's sister filling cups with ceremonial seeds (to commemorate DNA); and Elsa tending the stove. Rand showed up around four o'clock carrying, for my benefit, an enormous stack of obsolete space seder drafts and files. Bill, already dressed for the evening in dark slacks and a pressed sport shirt, joined Rand in the living room, where, the couch pushed back to make room for the banquet table, Bill's father Irv, shirtless, sang grumpy, anarchistic songs.

"Landing on the moon is the most profound event in the last hundred thousand years!" Bill started out my briefing, his fifty-year-old face blotchy with excitement. "That should be year zero! Note the millisecond Neil Armstrong put a foot on the moon! Restart the clock then! That is never to be repeated—the first step on another world! Men went through the transition of space and set foot on a heavenly body. It should be remembered, remembered thousands of years from now. So we wrote this seder to make sure nobody ever forgets. We'll tell the story, every year again, to the children. That way the event can be remembered for thousands of years, just like the events of Jewish history are remembered through the Passover seder."

The table had been set with candles, wine glasses, hard-boiled eggs, and perfect-bound Haggadahs—the seder text—each with a black-and-white picture of Neil Armstrong printed on the front. "Look, when you're a fish," Rand interrupted, "and you don't have lungs, the lack of water on land is a very big deal. But creatures figured out gradually how to start crawling onto land, eventually spending their whole lives here. They freed themselves from the bonds of the ocean. That was liberating for life, just as leaving the planet and freeing ourselves from the bonds of gravity is liberating for life. Think of it this way: we're literally stuck down on the planet, right? And the only way off is for us to achieve a velocity of 25,000 miles per hour. That's it! If you go 24,000 miles per hour, you'll be coming back. You'll go very far from Earth, but you'll be coming back. Turns out that at 25,000 miles per hour you just get over the hump to where you have positive outward velocity, when the effects of Earth's gravity diminish. You're free of the bonds of gravity!"

Rand inspected his black athletic shoes and ran his hands over his white-and-gray-patterned shirt. "The problem is, we have no way to achieve that velocity with anything we have right now. The Roton can't do it. The space shuttle can't do it. Nothing we've got today can do it. If we want to go back to the moon it'll take us about ten years! That's how long it took the first time! We're as far from breaking free of the bonds of gravity today as we were when Kennedy gave us the challenge."

At six o'clock, guests began arriving: a devout Christian space enthusiast, his dewy Montessori-teacher daughter, a young composer who the hosts hoped would score a space seder musical, the writer M. G. Lord, Rand's fiancée Patricia, and an assemblage of neighbors, including a seven-year-old girl named Anneka who had been doing this her whole life and, according to Rand, did not know this was a made-up holiday. Elsa laid out trays of chopped liver and capers. Then, just before sundown, everyone gathered around the table and sat down.

Bill, at the head, led the service as my own father had so many times throughout my youth. Bill, however, took liberties with the four questions, asking, "What is the significance of DNA?" ("DNA is the basis of life as we know it, and allows life on Earth to reproduce and evolve. It is found in the nucleus of every living cell"), and requesting we raise our glasses to the prophets Coulomb, Gauss, Ampère, Faraday, Maxwell, Kelvin, Joule, Carnot, Einstein, Curie, Bohr, Dirac, Heisenberg, and Schrödinger. The centerpiece of the ceremony was a transcript of the Apollo 11 lunar landing, painstakingly rendered by Bill and Rand. "Thirty-five degrees. Thirty-five degrees . . . Seven fifty, coming down at twenty-three . . . Seven hundred feet, twenty-one down, thirty-three degrees . . . Six hundred feet, down at nine-point-eight forward . . . Three hundred fifty, down at four . . ." The reenactment sounded nearly as gibberish-like as Hebrew. "Yes. Okay . . . CONTACT LIGHT . . . Houston, Tranquillity Base here . . . THE EAGLE HAS LANDED."

Moments after the guests left, Irv took his shirt off again and Elsa began vacuuming. I asked Rand if the bondage of gravity really impinged on his feelings of freedom.

"It definitely does," he said, wrapping up the leftovers of the infinity cake. "If I want to go to Nevada, I get in a car and go, and I would be very upset as an American if somebody told me I couldn't do that. And I'd be upset, even though I'm not physically capable because I don't have a rocket, if somebody passed a law saying I can't go to Saturn. Because that's a fundamental right. In terms of principle, nobody can tell me I can't go into space."

"But does the law of gravity feel like the same kind of law?"

"Yes," he said, preparing to head into the night. "Because it keeps me from going into space. I want to go into space right now. If I could go, I'd do it. But I can't—because Earth has too much gravity."

Gary's own form of prayer involved suspending his own disbelief and sustaining others' delusions. With Christmas coming on, spray-painted candy canes and snowflakes on the windows of the Mojave Wendy's, Gary tried to prepare his troops for Walt's up-coming visit by offering a simple, no-fault theory as to why we weren't yet in orbit. Not that everyone needed a mood lift. Brent, for one, was happier than ever. He'd recently returned from a sci-ence fiction convention in L.A., where he'd met a girl. "I ran into a guy from Pioneer the first night there," he told me, "and he was carrying a doumbeck"—a kind of drum—"and I asked him if he wanted to have a drum circle. So after the party in the hospitality suite we had a circle that ran for two-three hours, and this guy had a friend with him, a belly dancer, and she danced, and we all played, and eventually everyone's hands got tired and me and the belly dancer sat around talking." There was a hot tub, which they sat in until seven in the morning. Then they went out for break-fast. "She's a libertarian, pagan, belly dancer journalist," Brent described her, beaming. "She makes her own costumes. Damn."

Gary's seemingly insupportable doctrine rested on the tenet that the single greatest achievement in space history—the race to the moon—had, in fact, led to the space world's demise. Gary be-lieved that NASA, during the Apollo program, had botched the job completely. The media and the government mythologized the faithless, hyper-rational rocket scientist, and that myth, along, incidentally, with almost everything else to come out of NASA, was (a) philosophically untenable, and (b) a royal pain.

The Cold War, Gary started in, fixated the country on reaching the moon fast, not reaching the moon repeatedly, and the ramifications of that ran deep. The moon race, he argued, bastardized engineering practices. With space planes—the slower, more sustainable route to space; the route of choice until Kennedy's speech—gadgeteers could build a little, fly a little, build a little, fly a little, tweaking along the way. With ballistics—the quick, one-shot wham-bam shot to the sky—perfection was required right off the blocks. You had one chance: light the wick, see if the candle bombs or flies.

As Gary saw it, this conflict came to a head on October 15, 1957, ten days after *Sputnik I* first flew, when the country's top aerospace engineers convened at a prearranged meeting at Moffett Field. The goal was to finalize the shape of the X-20 spaceplane, the ridiculously named DynaSoar, a follow-up on the X-15. The DynaSoar was to fly to the edge of space, and theoretically, after it, the United States would build an aeronautically shaped space shuttle, and after that, a shuttle-like lunar ship. Or so everyone assumed until a prominent young engineer named Max Faget stomped out of the meeting, claiming he would not spend another minute on the DynaSoar or any other spaceplane, and anyone else who did was wasting his time. (Faget would later spend twenty years as director of engineering at the Johnson Space Center; he is credited with designing the Mercury space capsule, and he oversaw the Gemini and Apollo capsules and the space shuttle as well.) Ballistics, Faget insisted, was the way to beat the Russians. So he left, commencing work on his Apollo capsule immediately, pulling off a triumph of forbearance and showboatmanship that would plague Gary and the spacer community for quite some time.

Gary's second main gripe was that Apollo shifted heroes. During the moon race, the space diplomat ousted the lone-riding, spur-wearing test pilot. All men sent out of the stratosphere now represented God and country. Put a wild card—say, Chuck Yeager even—on the nightly world news, the front line of the Cold War, and who knew what he might say? That Yeager was the best test and fighter pilot this country had seen had no bearing. In World War II, he had shot down two German fighters in his first eight missions. In one session, he took out five German fighters in a row. But Yeager did not qualify to fly for NASA because, like a true Western folk hero, he lacked a college degree. Gary too had felt the brunt of NASA's snobbishness. Shortly after his Percheron blew up, the agency decided to nudge him out of the market, delivering to his prime investor a get-lost check. G. Harry Stine had reportedly overheard Max Faget say at a party, "The rocket business is no place for amateurs like Gary Hudson."

Though Gary was only a minor nuisance yipping at its ankles, NASA would have had many reasons to want him to stop. His ill-fated Percheron was the first privately funded space launcher in the country, and the ideal that launcher represented—the ideal of a purely commercial space sector—deeply threatened the once-golden agency that had lost its way. NASA had started gloriously, almost perfectly. Founded on October 1, 1958, with 8,000 employees, it had doubled in size within two years, and grown to 36,000 employees by 1966. During that same time, its budget had expanded eightfold, up to $5 billion annually, a staggering 4.4 percent of the national budget, 0.8 percent of the GNP. Between 1961 and 1975—tumultuous years for the country, to say the least—NASA completed the Mercury, Gemini, Apollo, Skylab, and Apollo-Soyuz programs, for a total of thirty-one consecutive expeditions without losing a single astronaut in space. (Three astronauts, however, died on the launch pad.) But the agency's heyday proved short-lived. By 1975, NASA's budget had dwindled down to one-quarter its Apollo peak. Layoffs started that same year, anathematic in an agency that had hired nearly 5,000 new employees annually from 1959 to 1967.

In going to the moon, the country spent a total of $24 billion—4 percent of the national budget for ten years. In the process, the United States erected what was then the world's largest building, the Vehicle Assembly Building at Cape Canaveral. It also contrived a permanent space bureaucracy, which in turn hatched space centers in California, Florida, Texas, and Alabama, bringing jobs to the Deep South. "If computers had been a government program," Gary lectured his lunch crowd at Wendy's, "none of you would have personal computers on your desks today, and if space remains a government program, none of you will get to go." Adding to the swampy legacy, over the course of Apollo, NASA dreamt up cost-plus contracting, a means by which Uncle Sam outsourced billions of dollars in hardware, offering no incentive for contractors to produce goods on the cheap. During the Saturn V program, the North American Aviation Company purchased and billed to the government a rosewood conference table so excessively large and elegant it appeared to float in midair. Why? Frugality would have met with diminished profits. Under cost-plus contracting the government asks suppliers only how much projects cost, and pays 8 percent on top of that.

Absurdly, NASA could not tolerate a commercial space sector—an industry that promised to give Americans the dream of space, in tax terms, for free—because public support for a government-funded moon shot had never existed in the first place. In May 1961, when Gallup pollsters asked Americans whether they would like to see their government "spend $40 billion—or an average of about $225 per person—to send a man to the moon," 58 percent of people responded no, 33 percent responded yes. By 1965, the ratio of people who wanted to see space spending cut to those who wanted to see it increased had risen to two to one. In 1967, just two years before the first moon landing, the president of the American Association for the Advancement of Science attacked the monstrosity of Apollo spending with considerable imagination and vigor, drawing up a list of what else the country could have done with $30 billion (his estimate of what Apollo spending would be). The roster: a 10 percent raise in salary, over a ten-year period, to every teacher from kindergarten through university in the United States (about $9.8 billion required); 50,000 seven-year fellowships, freshman through Ph.D., at $4,000 per person per year ($1.4 billion); a built and endowed university for all fifty-three U.N. member nations ($13.2 billion); three more permanent Rockefeller Foundations ($1.5 billion); donations of $10 million each to two hundred of the better small colleges ($2 billion); seed monies of $200 million each toward the creation of ten new medical schools ($2 billion); and the country would still have $100 million left over for informing the public about science.

Howard McCurdy, the public policy professor and space historian, wrote in *Inside NASA* (1993), "As NASA continued preparations for the lunar expedition, public support grew even weaker. It weakened as the United States prepared to go to the moon, it weakened as the United States went to the moon, and it weakened when the United States stopped going to the moon."

By 1973, over 85 percent of Americans wanted to see space spending drop. Space ranked below health, the environment, problems in cities, crime, drug addiction, education, and welfare in terms of popular support. NASA's approval ratings mirrored those of its least inspired sisters, the IRS and the FDIC.

After lunch—chased by vitamins, of course—Gary and his engineers drove back to Building 1, Gary to his drab claustrophobic office, furnished with a single chair and a small metal desk. The thin winter light failed to penetrate the windows; it diffracted off the blowing sand. No permanent computer here, Gary pulled his laptop out of his briefcase, logged on to the current e-mail debate—what color to paint the Roton; camouflage was a favorite, as was a yellow body with green lettering, to match the industrial supply catalog from which the engineers ordered hardware. Then he gathered his belongings and prepared to drive back home. "Walt's coming in a few weeks to see what I've been doing with his money," he said, playing his key chain nervously around his fingers. Outside in the parking lot, he stashed his briefcase and his duffel in the back seat and cued up five CDs in the changer in his trunk.

Brian—perhaps concerned that the Apollo program, a blatant success, struck his boss as such a failure—followed Gary to his car and asked him earnestly if he was okay. The wind howled, as it did most afternoons. Gary closed the car door. "There's a certain amount of introspection I will not do," he said, brushing off his pilot and turning over his engine. "The mind is a terrible thing to poke. I'd rather not look under that rock."

2

The first Rotary employee to lose faith and quit was Roger Houghton, the extremely skinny, bow-legged, and gimpy facilities manager, a weathered car-washing obsessive with a two-pack-a-day habit and a rented cottage behind White's Motel, where he slept on a mattress on the floor. As a young man in Florida, Roger had raced cars and motorcycles and never expected to live past thirty. When he did, he sold his 3,200 pounds of books, drove from Boca Raton to Mojave, and begged a job from Burt Rutan. That job lasted ten good years, until Roger hit "a long dark patch" during which his Porsche floated away in a flood. Then, in September 1998, Gary spotted Roger walking down the Mojave airport road, pulled over, and offered him work. Thus began Roger's stewardship of the Rotary Rocket hangars. He offered guests "the twenty-five-cent tour." It came with a free car wash and tune-up, and "a full money-back guarantee."

"I borrow a little and steal a lot," Roger had first explained his managerial philosophy to me in March 1998, limping around Building 31 in his moppy hair and Wrangler jeans. "Most of the desks I borrowed from places around the airport. We moved them very quietly, very late at night." Roger spoke in a strange and masking falsetto, like the wolf in Red Riding Hood's grandmother's clothes. "Initially," he twanged, "Gary wanted to buy a

$100,000 module, and I said just leave me alone." Roger brewed the coffee weak, installed swamp coolers instead of air conditioners, and, most unpopularly, rented a Johnny-on-the-Spot instead of plumbing a second bathroom. "We're trying to build a rocket here, not a luxury office building. If people don't want to be here, we don't want 'em. Mojave's the asshole of the universe, but it's the center of the world when it comes to wing-ed things."

Shortly after Thanksgiving, Roger could take no more of Gary's extravagant spending habits—the elaborate new phone systems, the deluxe high and low bays, the astronomical rents. He quit, but Rotary's absence left a gaping hole, and afterward he still hung out at the airport, detailing cars. At 8:30 one morning, I found him cleaning his engine with a toothbrush, an activity he'd already been at for two and a half hours. "Get your beauty rest?" he squeaked, handing me a mitt and some Soft Scrub, and popping open my Volkswagen's hood. He looked even skinnier than last time I'd seen him, his legs spindly under his jeans. "I think I'm going to buy me a motorcycle and drive it north, then drive it east, then drive it into Canada, then lash it to a train, then take that train west, then drive north to Alaska, and then come home." He spoke frantically, in a half-panic, trying hard to provide me with some exciting news, a new direction for his life. Eventually he swallowed hard, lay down on a dolly, slid under my car, and fell silent. "Usually I doze myself off at night by thinking of all the places I want to go. But lately it hasn't been working. All I really think about is driving fast."

What to believe in, what to yearn for, if not outer space? As Milan Kundera wrote in his novel *Slowness,* "Speed is the form of ecstasy the technical revolution has bestowed upon man. . . . There is a secret bond between slowness and memory, between speed and forgetting." A Nemesis Formula 1 race plane, tight and red, streaked overhead. We finished our cars, ate plates of pancakes at a diner, and then drove over to White's. "I'll be here all day," Roger said, parking, "taking all my chances." He sat down on his stoop and stared at his cuticles. "Actually, my big plan is to try to vacuum, but I'm not sure I'm even gonna do that."

3

Two weeks before Christmas, Walt arrived in Mojave in a Lear 35 jet. He wore a suede jacket over a Hawaiian shirt, and he traveled in the company of a couple of potential investors, a pair of brothers in their early thirties dressed in North Face jackets, running shoes, and shorts. The three disembarked on the flight line and hurried through the cold air into a Rotary van, which Gary navigated toward the Scaled Composites compound, attempting to ease tension by pointing out exotic planes. "That's a Voodoo F101," he said, deadpan. "That's a Navy C2, a cargo delivery plane." The air smelled heavy and metallic, laden with jet fuel. Walt checked his voicemail on his cell phone. "Those are F4 Phantoms. That's a baby C130," Gary said.

One of the running-shoed brothers interrupted, "What's the hardest part, getting up or getting down?"

"Both," Gary answered, still monotone. He added a pleasant non sequitur. "But we're not trying to do a research project here. We're trying to build a vehicle."

Inside the Scaled lobby, Burt Rutan greeted the guests and escorted them into his hangar, where his asymmetrical Boomerang hung upside down from the ceiling and his Proteus sprawled across the floor, that wide magisterial bird. "It's much cheaper for us to build a manned than an unmanned vehicle," Burt explained, handing out Proteus brochures. Walt climbed into the cockpit while Gary stood below. Then Burt steered the entourage over to the clunky black "ultimate Frisbee." The bottom piece of Gary's ATV, it was a twenty-two-foot-diameter carbon fiber disk, to be glued just below the LOX tank, where the engine was supposed to go.

Scaled's main workshop overflowed with resin, buckets, Kevlar scraps, foam dust, half-built shells of Pegasus rockets, and pieces of the X-38 Crew Return Vehicle, a lifeboat Burt had been commissioned to design for the ISS. In the clean room, Marti joined the group, handing the brothers halves of the LOX tank to hoist overhead. The crew cabin now stood assembled on the floor, a gumdrop-shaped pod roughly six feet in diameter with a round portal door. "We achieve static and dynamic stability by the Roton shape," Gary butted in, determined to be included. "We have a main engine which provides centerline thrust." Aircraft are controlled by aerosurfaces, like flaps, he explained. Rockets are controlled by thrusters. While the brothers stood with their ropy arms extended under the thin wide dishes, each weighing twenty-five pounds, Walt climbed in the cockpit and sat in one of the newly installed crash seats that Brian had scavenged, fiddling with the black molded control stick. Just before leaving, one of the brothers asked who was flying.

Marti raised a timid finger. "I'll be the one pushing the pedals," he said, "unless my wife really strenuously objects."

That afternoon—after a rather excruciating and poorly timed board meeting during which Rick Giarusso, who'd never succeeded in raising much money, was ousted in absentia as CFO—

Gary drove his visitors and Burt out to the test site, passing the padlocked bunkers, the gutted fuselages, the decaying crates of mysterious munitions, rocket bottoms like egg cups cooked by the sun. After a perfunctory safety lecture, we all walked over to the lip of the whirl stand pit, hardhats blowing off our heads, the brothers' exposed legs freezing despite the sun. "We're having some valve problems with the whirl stand preventing us from testing today," Gary announced, "but we can watch some early runs on video."

Inside the trailer, Burt sat cross-ankled atop a folding work table, his back flush against a poster of emergency contact numbers, his brown sandals revealing black-stockinged feet. As he cued up the tape, Gary, solicitous, asked Walt what color he'd like his Roton to be. But before Walt could answer, Burt interjected: "What did Henry Ford say? 'You can have it any color, so long as it's white'?"

4

By the time Gary mailed invitations to his rollout, in late January, his million-dollar high bay had risen out of the desert, brilliantly styled and delighted with itself, its purple-painted girders matching the purple hatch marks on its doors, the doors themselves double and sixty-five feet high, topped by a massive neon Rotary logo, the reds visible from the highway, swirling into the blues. The structure's size and clean lines suggested possibility, a huge modern improbable cube rising from the Joshua trees and sage. The doors slid apart dramatically, like the doors of an elevator, and the foundation contained an engine pit, dug out for quick-speed rocket oil changes, fitted with a hexagonal door. Gary understood well that people needed something to believe in, and he culled their belief using the same tactics used in high-end sales: aesthetics, charm, intelligence, nonchalance, originality, beauty, perseverance, a smooth tongue, and a surpassing and deeply disillusioned sense of human nature.

Early on in the Roton project Marti had whispered in my ear during an engineering meeting, "You realize this is art, don't you?" adding later, "How you can tell it's art is you give two groups of engineers a set of requirements and they come up with totally different designs." And now the ATV did resemble an art installation, the pieces refreshingly integrated and transcending their component parts: the igloo atop the rotor hub, the rotor hub atop the LOX tank, the LOX tank atop the payload bay, the payload bay beside the crew cabin, the two stacked together atop the kerosene tank, and the kerosene tank atop the Ultimate Frisbee, that proxy for the spinning engine disk.

The vehicle followed in a long line of nostalgic, futuristic spaceships—the Starship *Enterprise,* the *Millennium Falcon*—and like those artful cinematic props, it had been built cheaply with borrowed parts. Marti felt the process resembled the British import television show *Junkyard Wars.* The rotor blades had been stripped off an old S-58 helicopter; the rotor head off a different S-58 that had crashed its tail. The crew seats came from Vietnam-era Hueys, as did the control sticks. The auto-throttle was from a mangled Robinson R-22; the landing gear "oleos," or shock absorbers, from a nuclear sub. Even the "hardware in the loop" simulator—the flight-training computer that worked off inputs from the ATV's pedals, stick, and throttle—had been acquired in exchange for Marti's promising to co-write a paper and Gary's agreeing to place the proprietor's logo on the vehicle's side.

Eclectically stylish, the ATV possessed an obvious charm, but no sooner had Gary sent out his rollout invitations than he fell into a deep depression. Perhaps he felt the weight of his attempt to use an aerospace-world commonplace—the rollout of a new vehicle—to create a fantastical fiction—that common men would soon be traveling to orbit. "Things are okay," he said, "but I'm a pessimist." He rattled off a litany of grievances. He had not had enough sleep in several weeks. At the annual Anti-Aging Association convention, he'd been told his stress level was off the charts. For an FAA-sponsored conference, he soon had to return to the dreaded East Coast. His beloved Minnesota Vikings had missed the Super Bowl by only two games. The new CFO he wanted to hire—a Brit, Helena Hardman, a former JP Morgan telecom mergers and acquisitions associate—was being held up by the INS. His propulsion department had made almost no progress on the RocketJet engine. The so-called "adventure capitalist" Richard Branson had failed to respond to the pictures of a Virgin-emblazoned Roton flying over his private island. Worst, Gary had promised to roll out the ATV on March 1, and he would run out of money by April 1.

To lift his own spirits, Gary turned his attention not to the ATV, just down the road in his new high bay, but to the as-yet-unbuilt PTV, or the Propulsion Test Vehicle, which was not to be his next vehicle (that was the STV, or Structural Test Vehicle), but the vehicle after that, the one that would finally be able to fly to space. "Once Scaled is done with the PTV airframe, all we'll have to do is add the rotors and engine, if we maintain the option to do passive thermal control." He spoke in an escapist patter, to himself. "We can go with the passive approach if we use phenolic resin instead of epoxy resin. . . ."

From his briefcase, Gary produced a schedule showing the delivery dates of the ATV, STV, and PTV, the phases of development illustrated with white, black, and gray bars. His mood plummeted precipitously. "I look at the calendar here. I watch the days go by very, very quickly." He slid the schedule back in his bag and rubbed the corners of his eyes. "One of these days I need to really build a rocket. And I need to follow up with a few more names. Once I get into negotiations I have a reasonable success ratio." He rattled off a roster of the richest people he could think of. "I'm thinking maybe Paul Allen, Craig McCaw,

James Cameron, Dan Aykroyd. I need to bring in five or six million to get through the end of the year."

The second annual Federal Aviation Administration Commercial Space Transportation Forecast Conference took place over Valentine's Day in Washington, D.C., at the Washington Plaza Hotel, a steady and inoffensive establishment, its lobby decorated with knock-off Barcelona chairs, the walls various colors of beige. Just two weeks before Gary's rollout, all the usual suspects showed up—Buzz Aldrin, Pete Conrad, Robert Zubrin, Mike Kelly—plus the blue uniforms of the U.S. Air Force and gray suits from the FAA. The latter had long regulated rockets going up, but no agency had governed, or even considered governing, how they might come down. So this meeting was convened to address the gap—what level of risk was acceptable? What overflights should be allowed over populated areas? What kinds of system safety engineering processes should be used? Where should the abort sites be? Nearly everybody present had received a rollout invitation. "You can't show fear," Gary cautioned Marti, sitting in the main meeting hall.

Marti excused himself and returned five minutes later. "I feel so much better," he said. "I just threw up."

Throughout the former astronauts' opening remarks, Gary chattered nonstop—should Marti and Brian walk out of the high bay beside the ATV or sit in its cockpit? Should they alone wear the bright orange flight test suits, or should Gary wear one too? But when it came his turn to speak, he walked calmly across the pink carpet and stood at the podium. He repeated, as he had done so many times before, that the Roton would be piloted, with no mission control; just humans flying, doing their jobs, though they might, if the occasion arose, take some advice from the ground. Flight tests would begin in only two months. Marti, beside me, muttered to himself, "You want to know what it will really be like in space? It'll smell bad. It'll be very humid. A sealed cabin environment with one hundred percent recirculation, ninety to ninety-five percent of people throw up. That's why the cabin's pressurized. The only reason. There are two kinds of people in space: people who get sick and become incapacitated, and people who get sick and do okay."

That night, at the cash bar reception, a career government regulator informed me that the FAA's whole strategy here was ul-traconservative: to avoid "the Hindenburg effect," to prevent a single vehicle from bringing down an entire industry. "Like some of the concepts, what I want to know is, are they kidding?" He gestured with a toothpick from the free deli meats. "One of these concepts, maybe you know which one I'm talking about, has a *crew*. Okay, I acknowledge this needs to happen someday, okay? But we just got the authority to begin drafting rules to regulate reentry. So what I've got to say is, Whoa."

Modifying the old saw that you can't con an honest man, Gary had long since grown accustomed to brushing off his critics by hewing to the theory that you can't convince a man to believe in a spaceship who doesn't want to believe in a spaceship anyway. But the next day he suffered more than the usual attack when Marshall Kaplan, the chairman of Launchspace Publications and a former professor of aerospace engineering, delivered a lecture entitled "Basic Laws of Reusable Launch Vehicle Design," a summary of the weaknesses of the Roton project in the guise of an industry roundup. Kaplan stood with one leg straight and a hip thrust forward like a cocky teenage girl. Each of his seven laws pointed to something wrong with Gary's design, with the exception of the first, seemingly written purely to embarrass: "Lift-off of any vertically launched vehicle requires a thrust-to-weight ratio which is greater than one."

Under the conference hall's fake-crystal chandelier, Kaplan accused Gary of using the wrong fuel (kerosene instead of hydrogen), the wrong number of gears (four instead of three), the wrong number of stages (one instead of two), the wrong hardware (composite instead of aluminum), and the wrong business model (private instead of government-subsidized). Afterward he retreated to the hotel lobby. "One of three things will happen in the coming year," he told the small crew of loyalists who'd bunched around in Gary's defense. "One, Rotary Rocket will succeed—I give them a one percent chance, that would be fair. Two, they will evolve into something else. Or three, they'll go Chapter Eleven." He spoke with his eyes lightly closed, his belly jutting out toward his knees. "The Roton, how it is presently conceived and from what I heard yesterday, I give it zero chance of working."

"So why do you think Gary is building the Roton?"

"Hudson must be thinking one of two things," Kaplan replied. "He's either going to get money for this and build some other rocket with it, or he's committing some kind of fraud." The bystanders sputtered, infuriated. "He's either a hell of a salesman or he's a crook. Obviously it'll never work."

Fifteen minutes later the elevator doors slid back and Gary strode past the reception desk, hailed a cab, and headed toward the Air and Space Museum. The day felt cold and moist, Foggy Bottom flat and old, full of sober, predictable scenes. Wearing his long gray flannel topcoat, he leaned forward in the back seat, anxious, as if willing the car forward. I hadn't seen him at the lecture, though I'd carefully looked, but around Dupont Circle he declared, "I took that speech with a degree of pity. I was on the wrong side of the reusable launch issue for a long time, on the wrong side of popular opinion about what we should be doing in space, and so I know it doesn't feel very good to be in those shoes." His words spilled out in a rush. "A lot of stupid mistakes happen on the leading edge of technology. Sentries used to walk in front of the first automobiles carrying red flags because cars were thought to be very dangerous. People are always uncomfortable with the leading edge."

Just inside the Smithsonian entrance, Burt Rutan's Voyager hung like a Calder sculpture, a massive skeletal mobile of fragile limbs. Gary tucked his coat under his arm, as if to get to work. "The question is what we get to replace—the SS21 or the 20. . . ." He drifted across the atrium, staring toward the ceiling, shoulders spread wide as he scrutinized the Pershing missiles, each painted matte khaki and brutal gray. "I wonder if we'd fit under the mezzanine. I doubt it," he said, tapping two fingers against his lips. "Getting in here is like winning an Academy Award."

On the far side of the foyer, Gary dropped to his knees, pushed up his sleeves, and knelt before the Gemini and Mercury capsules, pointing out the radiating patterns on their round, black bottoms, the fittings, the seals, all burnt and bumpy, shockingly crude. "Frankly, looking at this gives me faith I can build the Roton." He rubbed his palms together. "The surface temperature here was probably 2,500 degrees. This stuff looks like it was put on by hand. Feel that. It's silicone, essentially bathroom caulk."

Upstairs, Gary lingered inside *Skylab,* reminiscing as if he'd lived there—here's where you throw your trash, that's the stationary bike that works, his musings far more cheerful than the astronauts who'd lived there, men who'd had to report every mouthful of food they ate, every urination, to catch and freeze-dry their own vomit, and to dry off with fire-resistant towels that felt like steel wool. Gary leaned over the mezzanine railing, studied again the long green SS-20 Saber, its multipart warhead nose. He squinted at the distance from its tip to the roof beams. "I really don't think we'll fit in here. They'll have to put us outside at the Cape."

The HL10, a metal coffin-shaped box dropped off a B-25 bomber, gave Gary "the willies." He lost focus staring at the complicated rig of mirrors that, even though only one and a half bells were present, reflected all five engines of the Saturn V. In the experimental zone, he dallied over the plug nozzle, a device that NASA said could not be built at all, and at the mock-up of the *Orion,* Freeman Dyson's tremendous phantasm that was to progress through space on nuclear charges. Finally Gary picked up a model of an A-2 rocket engine. It looked remarkably like the early Mojave engines. "I'd like to take a certain person who shall remain nameless here and show him this, and explain how I can make an SSTO"—single-stage-to-orbit rocket—"work ten different ways." Hands shaking, Gary set the rocket down, afraid he might drop it. "That is, if I was bothering to talk to him."

Over lunch, Gary rested his soupspoon after every few bites and dabbed drops from his chin. The sun hit low on the sheer glass wall, and his face looked older than the rest of his body, his palms so smooth and pink. "I think I could probably build the Roton," he blurted out, after a silence, as if we'd been having a conversation, "but it would be at the expense of my health. Raising money for the Roton is like the marching Chinese problem. If you try to march the entire population of China past a single post, you will never succeed. The line will always keep growing, people will always keep reproducing. There will always be more Chinese." What Gary was saying in his own cryptic way was that he knew he'd always need more money. He spent his money to raise more money. He could never raise enough. "Walt's done a tremendous thing for me, but now the kid's got to leave home."

On the mall in the dying winter light, Gary joined a stream of schoolchildren walking toward the Metro, but then he veered off, deciding to visit the tyrannosaurus at the Museum of Natural History instead. "I feel like I've aged four years in the past six months," he said. The late afternoon sky was the color of granite. The authoritarian Capitol rose at our backs. Gary wrapped his arms around himself, alone, seeking security. In just two weeks the entire space world would descend on Mojave. "I only feel young when I stand next to the rocket."

5

In the days before the rollout, the dream of Gary building a spaceship and the reality of his fabricating the world's tallest and strangest helicopter began to diverge. Nearly the entire Roton staff had quit engineering the rocket and switched to planning the party, spending days choreographing sound systems, fly-bys, bleacher installations, and caterers; renting popcorn carts and cotton candy machines, intended to lend the rollout a holiday feel. Brian said he felt like a housewife and Brent, still feeling great, kept running down Building 1 hallways, screaming, "We're absolutely not doing rocket science!" (He meant this as a positive, as if Rotary were only doing rocket engineering or "plumbing," not testing impracticable hypotheses.) "We're stealing results from NASA, from old German papers! NASA can't design an ablative pressure-fed engine as fast as we can!" Then he'd remember that, despite his newfound dating success, he was not working on the RocketJet engine at all but on the RocketJet engine display for the ATV rollout, and he'd settle for a more somber mood. "There's plenty of opportunity for somebody to die in this vehicle. If there's a peroxide leak it could start a fire in the airframe and blow up. But Marti and Brian would die with their boots on. I guess more catastrophic things could happen to them."

As a favor to Gary, I chauffeured down to the rollout the

elderly Max Hunter, a former weapons missile man, and his wife, Irene Manning, star of the 1942 movie musical *Yankee Doodle Dandy*. After graduating from M.I.T. in 1944, Max took a job with Douglas Aircraft, where he rose to the titles of Chief Missiles Design Engineer and Chief Engineer for Space Systems. Later he worked for Lockheed as Director of Advanced Space Systems and eventually wound up in *Newsweek* as the man behind Reagan's Star Wars. Over his career, Max had been responsible for the aerodynamic design of the Nike-Ajax and Hercules missiles, the general design for the Nike-Zeus missile, engineering oversight of the Delta and Saturn IV-S rocket stages, and management of the Hubble Space Telescope project. Simultaneously and very incongruously, he'd also pursued an interest in space tourism. In 1963, he published a paper entitled "Single Stage Spaceships Should Be Our Goal!" In 1989, he co-authored with Gary "A Reusable Commercial Space Transport in a World of Expendables: Development, Certification, and Operation." He also served, throughout the early 1990s, as the senior-statesman engineer on the Delta Clipper-X, a prototype reusable rocket, which first hovered on August 18, 1993, and last hovered on July 27, 1994, when a hydrogen explosion tore a large hole in its graphite-epoxy airframe's side.

Max and Irene lived in San Carlos in a split-level decorated with photographs of Irene with Humphrey Bogart and Cary Grant and a huge oil painting of Irene, circa 1945, visible from the front door. For the ride to Mojave she wore a fashionable black-and-white knit dress and enormous sunglasses to shield her failing eyes. "Dolly," she commanded her husband in her exacting, starlet voice, "Dolly, do you have my pillow? Dolly, I need my pillow!" Max was nearly deaf.

To break up the drive, we stopped for lunch at the terra-cotta cattle theme park Harris Ranch where, in the Western dining room, Irene grabbed her husband's hands and said, "Thank you, Lord, for bringing us all together and for carrying us safely, safely, safely on our drive." Then she added, "Nobody remembered Irene Manning after she got back from five years in England. They should have remembered Irene Manning."

On the road again, Irene slept through the indignities of Bakersfield while Max wondered aloud when rockets had stopped being dead-serious business, when they'd switched from being instruments of war into toys for play. "That's how they were, you know, when I was young," he said. "We were always in a hurry. Our necks were always on the block." Max dozed off in the altitude of Tehachapi Pass, then roused as we drifted into the desolate flats of Mojave. The huge white high bay with its Rotary logo dominated the horizon. Max smiled slowly and rocked his head. "Gary will be hysterical if he ever gets anything into orbit."

The town teemed with old American sedans, lonely men driving them, and across the paved weave of decrepit houses rose the sheer cube, its sign shining proudly, like a false sun. The high bay itself looked as enticing as a gift box, and inside, exceeding all expectations, stood the most spectacular toy. The height! The halo of rotors! The rocket sleek and white, with gray and red accents, a vertical ladder of cut-out footholds leading to the round cabin crew door. For the occasion, Gary had rented a set of purple-draped flight stairs, the exact same purple as the high bay's girders, against which, on the vast back wall, loomed an enormous American flag. Thus installed, the ATV looked like a truly spectacular object, an enormous, almost architectural icon, a kin of the HOLLYWOOD sign in the Los Angeles hills, an engineering expression of a radiant American dream. (As Sol LeWitt wrote, "Conceptual artists are mystics rather than rationalists. They leap to conclusions that logic cannot reach.") Several large stickers adorned the vehicle's side: an American flag, the golden bear of the California state flag, and the vehicle ID number, N990RR.

The next day, friends and family day, the dress rehearsal for the rollout proper, Brent milled about holding hands with his belly-dancer girlfriend Dawn; Christopher—who'd recently moved from Cal City to Mojave; too many scorpions—escorted his father; and Helena Hardman, the new mid-thirties CFO, spun in circles by herself, trying to grasp her job's remarkable complexities. Gary's parents showed up as well, his father, Noble, in pointy cowboy boots, a deep green suit, and a yellow polo shirt buttoned all the way to the top; his mother, Marcella, sweet-faced and diminutive, with white curly hair and a brown leather jacket the same color as her son's. Outside, an army of laborers erected an amphitheater of bleachers. Inside the low bay, caterers arranged salads, beach balls, umbrellas, and driftwood, creating a nostalgic beach-party tableau. Gary, channeling both Barnum and Buck Rogers, had transformed the high bay itself into a space travel museum. Purple-and-white-clothed tables flanked the tow-ering walls. On each stood a sign that addressed concerns sure to be on visitors' minds.

HOW DOES THE ROTON OPERATE?

1. CARGO LOADING A typical Roton flight begins in the high bay (where you are standing) with the loading of cargo into the Roton. This is followed by rollout to the launch pad.

2. FUELING & CREW BOARDING At the launch stand, the Roton is fueled and prepared for flight. The crew boards the vehicle and conducts preflight checkout procedures.

3. LAUNCH & ASCENT The crew initiates the launch sequence and the vehicle takes off vertically, powered by its rotary RocketJet™ powerplant. It flies to orbit using standard global positioning system (GPS) and inertial navigation flight control systems. The crew monitors operations.

4. CIRCULATION Following main engine cutoff at about a 70 NM altitude, the Roton circularizes its orbit using its orbital maneuvering thrusters. In orbit, the vehicle has a maximum stay of 72 hours.

5. CARGO DEPLOYMENT On orbit, the cargo is verified as operational and is deployed. The crew does some sightseeing until they are ready to return to Earth.

6. DEORBIT Before the Roton performs its reentry burn to deorbit, the four rotor blades are deployed. During the hypersonic and supersonic phases of flight, the base of the vehicle produces most of the drag while the rotors remain windmilling behind the vehicle, stalled in the airflow, helping to stabilize the vehicle until it reaches subsonic speed.

7. AUTOROTATION At an altitude of about 28,000 feet, the rotor is sped up using the passing airflow and the blades begin to produce lift such that the vehicle enters autorotation. With a glide ratio of 1.5:1, the pilot is able to fly five nautical miles at a relatively slow 45 knots, directing the Roton to a precision landing point.

8. TIP ROCKET POWERED LANDING Just prior to landing at about 500 feet, the rotor blade tip thrusters are fired, allowing the pilot to make a powered landing.

9. TURNAROUND After landing, the vehicle undergoes minor maintenance and checkout procedures for its next flight, usually within two days.

And:

THE ROTON IS AN AIRCRAFT

The Roton design is based on the commercial aviation model, which has provided a successful template for aircraft-based transportation systems. The Roton design benefits from the following commercial aircraft attributes:

- *Full Reusability, Single-Stage*
  All aircraft have this obvious characteristic because it reduces pre-flight costs; only fuel is consumed during flight.

- *Multiple Engines*
  Like commercial aircraft, the Roton is designed to operate safely on a reduced number of engines in case of malfunction.

- *Piloted*
  Autopilot with human intervention capability is key to ensuring the safe operation of both the Roton and commercial aircraft.

- *Low Maintenance Costs*
  Aircraft are turned around quickly between flights because they are simple to maintain; the Roton is designed to enable minimum turnaround delay.

- *Low Support Infrastructure*
  The Roton, like aircraft, will require minimal on-the-ground support and infrastructure (e.g. fueling, cargo handling).

- *Abort Capability*
  The Roton will use traditional aircraft technology and architecture to enable recovery from most system and component failures.

Like the big tent, the rollout featured real-world feats of skill, focus, and contortionism, involving elaborate makeup and sleight of hand. Derivative of the Smithsonian's Saturn V display, an elaborate set of mirrors reflected the twenty-two-foot-diameter, ninety-six-combuster rotating engine, which Gary hadn't yet built. Televisions looped black-and-white footage of 1950s and 1960s NASA wind-tunnel rotor tests. A computer screened a simulated Roton landing, the rocket rotating down from six nautical miles, making a ninety-degree turn left, then gliding toward the pad, firing up the tip rockets at 500 feet and making a spot-on touchdown.

On a table near the rear lay a high-temperature rotor blade, or a mockup of a concept of a section of a blade, as not even the materials for the blades existed yet.

HIGH TEMPERATURE BLADE SECTION

The rotor for the Roton must survive the heat generated while entering the atmosphere, which can produce a maximum temperature of 2500°F. This mockup shows a concept for a spaceworthy blade. The spar in this model is made of aluminum, but the actual Roton will use a standard, commercially available titanium helicopter spar that has been proven in hundreds of thousands of flight hours. The spar is insulated from reentry heating by a high temperature composite blade section that also acts as the trailing edge of the blade. These sections are made of a composite material [unnamed] that actually gets stronger when heated and can withstand 6000°F.

The most outlandish installation was the Orbital Transfer Vehicle, or UpStage OTV, a piece of proprietary technology I'd never heard of before, represented by a large-scale "conceptual model": several large drums covered with reflective tinsel.

CONCEPTUAL MODEL OF
ORBITAL TRANSFER VEHICLE (OTV)

This model represents one module of the UpStage OTV, which takes payloads from low earth orbit (LEO) to destinations at higher altitude. UpStage modules are delivered to LEO separately by the Roton, and then docked to form a stack of any required size. This system can deploy spacecraft of virtually any type, including small devices in LEO, the largest comsats in geosynchronous orbit (GEO), and spacecraft aimed at the moon.

A long line snaked down the flight stairs from the ATV itself, all the Rotary employees, their friends and families waiting their turn to sit in the vehicle and try their hands at the cockpit controls. Gary too queued up, accompanied by his own parents, Anne along with them wearing Chinese pants and a tank top, a fake tattoo on her left shoulder, her hair dyed auburn red. Gary's bald spot had grown to the diameter of a baseball. He hadn't been in Mojave in several weeks. Anne nudged him gently to cut ahead in line.

Up the steep purple stairs, onto the landing, and into the gumdrop crew cabin, Gary settled next to Marti into an upholstered crash seat, where he fingered the red bomb release and turret gun trigger buttons on the Cobra helicopter stick. A hatchet, sheathed in a leather case—in the event the ATV tipped on its face and the pilots needed to hack apart the airframe to escape—hung on the wall over his shoulder. Gary focused on the heads-up display as he worked the stick, throttle, and pedals. On the screen before him, the simulated rocket barrel-rolled, vertically, nauseatingly.

"I trust you're better at flying this thing than I am," Gary said, shaken, after crashing for the third time.

"I both think and hope I am, sir." Marti nodded.

Gary gripped the flight stair railings. Everyone clapped as he stepped down.

In Gary's defense, the Roton ATV was alarmingly difficult to fly. Helicopter flight is governed by the pitch, or the angle, of the rotor blades as they sweep through the air. For climbing and descending, that pitch is changed at the same time and at the same degree—increased for up, decreased for down—and because it is changed collectively, this control is known as "collective." For forward and backward flight, the pitch of blades is increased at one specific point on the rotor hub's circular pathway, or cycle, so this is termed "cyclic." To take off in a helicopter, one powers up the blades (using the throttle), rotates the blades up to bite into the air (using the collective, controlled by the right hand), and then adjusts the blades to bite more over the vehicle's back than its front (using the cyclic, controlled by the left hand), causing the helicopter to move forward. The feet work the pedals, which are connected to the tail rotors—or in the ATV's case, to the rear-mounted, peroxide-powered thrusters—to turn the vehicle right and left.

Test pilots rate how difficult an aircraft is to fly using the Cooper Harper rating, a scale from one to ten. A one means an aircraft is simple to fly; a ten means an aircraft is so difficult to fly a crash is virtually guaranteed. At Gary's request, over seventy-five test pilots from military and civilian test pilot schools tried their hands at the ATV simulator, and even after a day of practice all of them rated the ATV a ten. Marti and Brian stood a twenty-dollar bet to the first person who, after a day of practice, could take off and land the ATV without crashing. They never had to pay out.

The ATV was cumbersome for many reasons, including its strange elongated shape. In flight characteristics it resembled a fire-fighting helicopter dangling a full sling of water—its low center of gravity made it want to swing like a pendulum. Worse, the tip rockets took over a second to react to any changes in the throttle, and the rotor was unstable in speed. An increase in the blades' RPM would cause the tip rockets to produce more thrust, which in turn would make the RPM soar even higher (this was worrisome because over-speeding could cause the blades to fly off), and the spinning forces also compounded as the RPM wound down. Most disconcerting, unpowered or autorotated landings unnerved even the most seasoned pilots. Brian once remarked that more people died practicing emergency unpowered landings than were saved by the ability to perform them. Thus both he and Marti spent long hours working on the simulator, rehearsing the foot and hand gestures required for the flight tests, now less than eight weeks away.

At dusk, with the winds at seventeen knots and gusting to thirty—blasts much stronger could have tipped the Roton over—Gary initiated his rollout rehearsal, complete with the anthems and dry ice. Marcella, Noble, and Anne all sat huddled in the bleachers while Gary stood alone, feet parted for balance, as the speakers blared Copland's *Fanfare for the Common Man* and the high bay's huge white doors divided, exhaling clouds of steam. Thirty years had come to this—a snub-nosed Caterpillar chugging forth from the fog, the ATV trailing behind, white and tall with red and gray accents, on a pier of canary-yellow wheel jacks. Everyone applauded openly, earnestly, at this sight they craved.

"So there it is," Gary said, apathetic.

One of the rotors hit a high bay door as it rolled back in.

Speeding over to White's, steering frantically through the airport's darkening streets, Gary broke into a rendition of *Henry V,* "Once more into the breach, dear friends, once more. . . ," the grandiose monologue in which the beleaguered King Henry attempts to rally his doomed troops. "Or close the wall up with our English dead!/In peace there's nothing so becomes a man as modest stillness and humility:/But when the blast of war blows in our ears,/Then imitate the action of the tiger;/Stiffen the sinews, summon up the blood;/Disguise fair nature with hard-favor'd rage;/Then lend the eye a terrible aspect." Anne caught her husband's gaze, as if expecting the dramatics to end, but they carried on: "My ransom is this frail and worthless trunk;/My army but a weak and sickly guard!"

The moon hung low, as yellow as a street lamp. White's entire parking lot was full. Slipping into the last remaining space, Gary asked Anne if she felt lucky. Anne sighed and averted her eyes, unsure what to say.

Room 269 was, according to Roger White, "the presidential suite," though it suffered the same cigarette-burned carpet and checkerboard table as all the rest. Gary uncorked a bottle of Wild Hare Merlot, tipped a long pour into a plastic bathroom cup, and flopped onto the springy bed. "I've finally figured out what I need to do," he announced, wedging two pillows behind his neck. "I need to spend more time in Mojave. I need to fire two-thirds of my employees. I also need to find a replacement for myself. I'm going to have to make some serious decisions in the next two weeks." Anne rummaged in her purse for a bag of white and mint-green capsules, which she swallowed with a bright orange soda. "I'm a really good idea man, and I'm a decent systems engineer, but I'm really not much of a businessman. I hate running companies. In fact, I'm pretty miserable running this one. I've been training to run this company all my life."

This was welcome news, a major insight into a thirty-year cycle Gary would have done well to break. Sliding on his half-cut glasses, he pulled a nine-page manuscript out of his pants pocket to rehearse for tomorrow's speech. "The modern version of this dream is now one hundred years old. . . ." His voice trailed off, tremulous.

He tossed aside the paper and the pillows, and lowered his head. As I left, he said to expect steady winds with dangerous gusts for the following day.

At seven o'clock the next morning, the Scaled crew began filling the ATV's peroxide tanks with water to lower the vehicle's center of gravity and thus prevent it from tipping over. About a thousand people turned out, mostly press, spacers, and Gary's rocket-fanatic competitors. Everyone received Roton name tags and embroidered Rotary valise bags. Then they were shepherded into the bleachers, where, in the torrential wind, they awaited the awkward concealed beast.

Pete Conrad—feisty, compact, with his big-weekend grin and gap between his teeth—sweet-talked himself into a pre-curtain viewing, strutting into the high bay like a general, saying, "Look at that, they got it all painted up anyhow." Conrad had gone down in space history not only for his Apollo-era "Enema Bag Showdown," during which he'd said in the Air Force's Lovelace Clinic, "General Schwichtenberg, you're looking at a man who has given himself his last enema," but for his scrappy command of the first *Skylab* crew. Now, up in the cockpit, Brian oriented the former astronaut. "The sim has you start at eight thousand feet, four miles, so what you need to do is make a left-hand turn descending. I'll start it, give you a little flavor of what it's like, and then we'll trade spots."

Conrad fidgeted, feet barely reaching the pedals, while Brian, working the simulator, landed the vehicle once and then again. When the former astronaut took the controls, he crashed the

ATV twice within forty-five seconds. Back on the ground, he shook Gary's father's hand. "Your son's doing a great job here," Conrad said.

"That boy," Noble replied, "was born with his head in the clouds."

Who could have imagined it would come to this—Scaled commissioned to fabricate a simulacrum, and a great crowd arrived to see a model rocket rolled out? A squadron of F4 Phantoms flew overhead. Three wrens chased one another above the wind-blown crowd. Again, the Peavey amps blared *Fanfare for the Common Man,* and just moments before the rollout's scheduled eleven o'clock start, Walt touched down. Tom Clancy too landed with only minutes to spare, emerging smoking, wearing camouflage pants and a railroad engineer's hat, walking with his buxom, full-lipped fiancée, reporting to anyone who would listen, "She's the one all the blonde jokes are about. And she's twelve times as rich as me!"

The ghostly financier took a seat alongside Baboo, the Sikh, and a tall skinny woman in heels and a black dress. Mike Kelly, whose own Eclipse had not yet been built, muttered, watery-eyed, "This is a great day for everybody, for the entire space community, but especially for Gary." The event felt spectacular, predestined, like Don King's "Rumble in the Jungle," though tortuous and emotionally confusing. Gary continued to hide out behind the bleachers, out of everybody's line of sight, and at a quarter past eleven, Rick Tumlinson, the rabble-rousing president of the Space Frontier Foundation, stepped in front of the high bay to warm up the crowd. "Welcome to the revolution!" he screamed, as if at a political convention. "Nobody told me the revolution would look like a traffic cone with helicopter blades on top, but there it is! This is the revolution! This is a myth-shattering machine!"

Gusts seared the microphone, making it nearly impossible to hear. Tom Clancy kissed his fiancée and snuffed out his cigarette. "I've known Gary nine years now," he began without notes, unprepared, "and I realized within three minutes that this was a guy with a dream. *Impossible* means we can't do it. We call them Luddites. We call them idiots. Our country has been here two hundred fifty years. We've invented everything that's useful in the world. The reason I'm wearing this hat"—he pulled off his blue and white railroad engineer's cap—"is that this is the train that's going to space. This is the Union Pacific railroad, the steam engine that opened the West. History starts today. Right here. Thank you."

The speech ended abruptly, and after a long silence Gary finally stepped forward. Playing the reluctant hero, he informed the crowd that he'd decided not to give his nine-page talk. "All you need to know is that we're going to take off from right there"—he pointed toward the test site—"about 3,000 feet, and land right there"—he pointed toward Cal City—"about 1,000 feet." His voice sounded Midwestern, laconic and trustworthy, not egomaniacal. He sloughed off honors, and with them responsibility. "The credit belongs to the people who have had this dream for a hundred years: Tsiolkovsky, Goddard, Oberth. Bevin McKinney is the first name on the patent, and it belongs there. And let me just say one more thing: we're going to roll the vehicle out of the high bay, and then we're going to roll it right back in."

Noble clasped his hands together over his mouth. Marcella gazed up at the sky. From the steam, the fantasy of the dry ice, Marti and Brian emerged as heroes, dressed in bright orange flight suits, striding somberly beside the great aerodynamic chariot, its base flared, its nose pointing up to that alluring ceiling of blue. The test pilot costumes looked perfect: zippers everywhere, just one patch, last names embroidered across left chest pockets, pegged slim legs tucked into black combat boots. Once the entourage cleared the high bay doors, Gary joined the aces. He shook their hands, then fell in line, the amphitheater exploding in cheers. The entire crowd knew what it was looking at—an extremely cumbersome helicopter, two former Navy pilots—but the vision was simply too much to resist. Marti and Brian really did look like astronauts, the ATV like a spaceship, and in the next few months these men and this vehicle would begin their tests: first a tie-down test, then a hover test, then a flight down the runway, and finally an up-and-over trajectory, during which the two pilots would climb the machine up to 2,000 feet, kill the power to the rotors, and try to land.

The vehicle already held several records: the tallest and most fuel-consuming helicopter ever built, and the largest composite airframe in private hands. Inaudible to the crowd, Gary whispered in Brian's ear, "Oh Lord, I know not what I have done." Bevin joined the processional, followed by Gary's parents. Anne then greeted her husband in an exuberant if weary embrace.

After the press snapped pictures—though not of Walt ("Being famous will not significantly improve my life. I'll be there when it comes time to collect the profits")—the Caterpillar dragged the Roton back inside. When the high bay doors closed, those of the low bay next door opened, revealing Caesar salad, shrimp cocktail, meats of all sorts, French pastries, diamond-shaped brownies, Roton-shaped chocolates, an elaborate spread. Every half hour, from noon until five, a bright yellow school bus pulled out from the flight line to bring visitors to tour the test site. Every three minutes, a new guest ascended the flight stairs and buckled himself into the ATV. After all he'd spent on the party, Gary had funds for only one month of operation—not enough "to put some air under the gear," to get the flight tests off the ground. The rollout was an act of extravagant folly, both personally and financially, a gala ball for a junkyard rocket that could never fly.

"Nobody will ever invest in Rotary," Walt said, boarding the Lear 35 and preparing to taxi away. "Only a fool like me would, because it makes no sense."

The day proved deliriously fun and entirely ridiculous, the biggest spacer party of the post-Apollo era. Throughout, Gary kept disappearing for disturbingly long stretches of time. His parents retired early to White's, worn out from relief and the enduring strain. Max Hunter never summoned the energy to climb up into the crew cabin. His wife bellowed a high C below the cockpit, but still nobody remembered Irene Manning. Max said, "Maybe I'm just an old geezer, but I'm having a hard time understanding Gary's point with this darn thing." He closed his eyes, profoundly tired, and at the first signs of dusk he asked me to drive him home.

PART
THREE

1

Come April, with the drying spring winds and the fleeting poppy season over, all the color washed out of Mojave. The semis still parked in the streets. Young boys still curled up asleep on AstroTurf-covered porches. Jackrabbits, ears as big as shoes, still hopped into cracked open fuselages, froze, and stared. A vulture perched in the cockpit of *Embraceable Amy*, a big white amputated private airliner missing several layers of skin. For solace, one could turn only to the improbable Mojave Movements Dance Studio, the six-dollar haircuts, the Bible study groups, the shimmering bands of heat. Kids dragged each other through alleys on wheeled red carts. The air smelled nice when it rained.

Gary drove to Mojave only once that early spring, and though he persisted at courting Richard Branson—mailing the Virgin CEO ever more Rotons with Virgin logos on their sides—he changed nothing and fired nobody, including himself. The only real money to come out of the rollout was $3 million more from Walt, enough to fund the flight test program through the end of June. So while Marti and Brian prepped for the tests, Gary instructed his accountant to cut any and all costs, which resulted in selling off the company cars, charging thirty-five cents for sodas and candy bars, and asking all employees to defer part or all of their pay. Christopher and some of the younger guys took to driving to L.A. on weekends, seeking the more immediate, more reliable pleasures of pools, girls, and beer. Meanwhile, Gary and his veterans retreated further into themselves. "It's never going to be fully baked, but at least it's half-baked," one of them said, the words spilling through a bright upsetting smile. He patted Gary on the back. "You've always said, at a year from money"—a year from earning revenue—"we needed to have something that looked like it could leave the ground. That's always been the plan, right? And that's what we've got here. Whether it can leave the ground is a detail."

In the weeks preceding first flight, Marti trained by flying a wide range of helicopters, often dangling a weight on a sixty-foot line, always wearing a strange, visor-like contraption he called his "nun's habit," a headpiece with white blinders blocking peripheral vision as it would be blocked in the ATV. The inside of the vehicle had begun to resemble a secret fort—the interior walls black, ledged and waffled; the floor concave and studded with scuba bottles installed to pressurize the crew cabin. To get inside the cone, one had to scuttle across the high bay floor and poke up through a hole in the bottom of the ultimate Frisbee. From there, a red stepladder rose up to a mossy green mixer box, which sent inputs from the control sticks up to the rotor blades. Out of the mixer box extended four chartreuse rods, each curving over the crew cabin, then running to the airframe's top. Marti stood inside the cone with several Scaled technicians, floppy hat on his head, hands on hips. "My wife keeps saying," he rationalized, " 'You're not going to fly this thing. You're going to kill yourself. You guys don't know what you're doing.' But every time she brings up a problem, I understand that problem and have thought of it already." He turned to one of the techs. "The big thing I ask for from you is no free play in the stick. Having that in a helicopter is devastating." He looked toward me. "*Devastating.* Is that the right word?"

Brian quelled his fears by instilling an iota of military discipline, insisting everyone show up for work by nine A.M., a huge imposition to Gary's senior employees, most of whom liked to stroll in sometime after ten. I found him dressed in a United States Naval Test Pilot School T-shirt, feet propped on his desk, elbows extended wing-like behind his head. "Yeah, I'm itching to fly, but a crash would be catastrophic with the stuff that thing's made out of. Hardly a day goes by when I don't bounce between thinking, 'This should be fun, very smooth,' and to the other side, 'My God, we really haven't looked at this here, the questions of aerodynamics, we rushed the simulator for the rollout, made it artificially easy—God, I would really like more time.' " One of Brian's sons had built him a LEGO Roton ATV crew cabin, complete with two crash seats and a heads-up display. It sat on his bookshelf, between the panorama of the King's Park golf course and the snapshot of the Russian MIG crashing into the earth.

"With ground resonance, once the vehicle starts to wobble, it could easily roll itself over in less than five seconds. But we don't want to get into an analysis paralysis situation. In the Navy, you spend about the equivalent of a month doing practice carrier landings on the runways before ever going out to the ship. And stopping at this point would be like completing the workup cycle and then not going to the ship. Anyone you approach to support your career choice as a naval aviator will want to know why you're still landbound. We used to call people like that seagulls—a lot of noise and flapping, but when it came to carrier landings they disappeared with colds and other ailments. So I guess what I'm trying to say is we're kind of at that point where we have to go boldly. . . ."

By mid-May, the rotor blades had been balanced on the ATV, the tip rockets had been mounted, and Richard Branson, international playboy, flew to Mojave. The timing was good, in that Branson had recently trademarked the name Virgin Galactic Space, and he'd scheduled a massive kickoff party for www.virginmega.com in L.A., complete with *Playboy* and television reporters following him around. When his King Air landed in Mojave, a *60 Minutes* crew had already installed itself in Building 1, allowing them to catch the adventure capitalist as he entered, charismatically unkempt, with bloodshot eyes, rumpled hair, and a short-sleeve button-down shirt untucked in the back. Helena—British, young, and attractively bored-looking—clutched at his elbow, leading him down the hallway. "Isn't he good-looking?" she whispered to me en route. "He's just so good-looking I can't believe it."

Gary had instructed his crew to decorate the conference room with the rollout displays, the posters describing the High Temperature Blade Section and the Conceptual Model of the Orbital Transfer Vehicle (OTV), the screens playing vintage NASA wind tunnel footage and animated Roton landings. Gary began the meeting as if this were A.A. "I'm Gary Hudson, and I've been trying for thirty years to build a single stage reusable spaceship." He listed his upcoming Roton variations—ATV, STV, PTV, PTV-2—then added darkly, "We know everything about this business. We know where all the bodies are buried—ha!"

Branson, clearly hungover, listened with a finger stuck in one ear. He asked only a single question after forty minutes: "What do you think your chances are of getting to orbit?" He then hammed it up for the *60 Minutes* crew. "Because, obviously it's a very good business if you can get it up."

After lunch at Denny's—during which a child pestered Branson with a dollar bill to sign—Gary drove the billionaire over to the low bay, where he'd installed a couple of propulsion engineers dressed up in greasy rubber aprons, taking apart rocket combusters like historical reenactment docents. Burt Rutan, with his stealthy but keen business sense, showed up in his Birkenstocks, his Proteus parked outside, visible through the low bay door. "We're taking her to the Paris air show next week," he said to Branson, nodding. "It's the first time we'll take her across the pond."

Gary stood a few yards away, the corners of his mouth turned down. Straining toward decorum, Branson said to Burt, "I guess I'll ask what chance you think the Roton has to succeed."

Burt responded sharply, "First, I guess I'll ask you what chance you think they'll get funded."

Mid-afternoon, Gary finally boosted Branson up into the crew cabin for an actual "test." Since the rollout, a fine white powder had coated everything in the high bay, making the radios, the fire extinguishers, the telephones, even the lunch boxes look relic-like and old. The fancy purple flight stairs still led to the cockpit, and the enormous American flag still hung on the back wall. But one of the ATV's side panels had been removed, marring the Rotary logo. Dusty, in pieces, the vehicle no longer appeared inevitable. It seemed flawed, vulnerable, private even, like a half-made-up starlet, like a dream described out loud after you awake.

The day's test was a plumbing test. Special ion-free water would be used to purge the rotor tip-rocket system, causing the rotor blades to spin and produce a very loud noise. Each of the four tip rockets weighed nearly four pounds, and had a thrust-to-weight ratio of 230 to one. During actual flight, hydrogen peroxide and sodium permanganate would be injected into the chambers, reacting and expanding out through the nozzles at supersonic speeds. Today, however, no chemicals would be injected, no gases would expand, and Branson sat motionless in the cockpit, hands on his knees, while Marti worked the controls. Back on the ground, the billionaire scrunched his brow and tousled his hair, confused. "So this is basically just a helicopter, isn't it?" he asked. The rotors kept whirling slowly, raining water. Everyone's ears continued to ring from the deafening boom.

Ever polite, Branson stuck around long enough for Helena's surprise birthday party, during which Gary presented him with a 3-D scale model Roton and a Dixie cup of champagne. Shortly after the cake, Branson excused himself, kissing the birthday girl on the cheek. "Darling," he said, apologetic, passing on to her the palm-size model round-nosed cylinder, "I think all it does is vibrate."

2

Early June, Walt's three million draining quickly, flight tests still weeks away, Gary slumped, defeated, in his Silicon Valley office, clearly losing his mind. Along the bay the leaves formed a sweet light canopy in the salty-fresh air, but inside the tinted windows cast a grayish pall, one well-suited to Rotary's dismal state of affairs: no coffee bar built, no side suites subleased, just Gary hemorrhaging $45,000 monthly for six times as much space as needed. The FAA still had not issued the ATV's Airworthiness Certificate, and just yesterday Gary had returned from Korea on a fruitless fundraising mission. "I really don't like my current job," he said from behind his horseshoe desk, speaking so baldly it made me nervous. "Many times I question whether or not it's worth it. How much damage can a vision do? I've led a great many people astray."

Gary's office now included not only models of the Liberty and the Percheron rockets, but also a can of Virgin Cola (Branson had declined to invest), a dust jacket from *Kings of the High Frontier* (the science fiction novel that featured Gary thinly fictionalized as the dashing Gerald Cooper), and transparencies of early bladed Rotons—this last a prematurely fatalistic, backward-looking move. "I'm stretched to the edge," Gary said, sinking so low in his chair he threatened to disappear. "Since I've started this project I've gained five, eight pounds. I have a treadmill at home I've got no time to use. I can't do this much longer, I need to pace myself." He clutched his hands around his head, as if to stop it from spinning. "I've got to get a big score. I need to spend $3.2 million a month to have a chance of flying sub-orbital by the end of next year, or at least 2 million a month to be running hard and fast." He righted himself and picked up a copy of the *Forbes* magazine in which he'd recently been profiled. The same issue had included a roundup of billionaires—Gary had sent Roton videos and Rotary Rocket prospectuses to them all. "What I want to say to all these people," Gary said, slamming the magazine against his desk, "is, 'Where have you people been?' Grab them by their throats until their heads pop off."

Spent, Gary closed his eyes and tried to slow his breathing. But when I asked what he planned to do now, he exploded, overwrought. "I don't want to look under that rock!" he insisted, then paused. "Did you ever see that movie *The Last Starfighters*? There's this scene in it where the bad guy aliens are about to crash into an asteroid, and there are two guys on deck. They've exhausted everything, they're clearly going to crash, and one of the bad guy aliens says to the other, 'What do we do now?' And the other alien says, 'Now we die.'"

I tried to console Gary, unsuccessfully, with my theory that the journey of building the Roton, the opportunity to spend one's lifetime trying to build a spaceship, working on a dream, was its own reward. He seemed to buy none of the koans so popular with his wife—to travel hopefully is better than to arrive; pain is inevitable, suffering is optional. "I sometimes wonder why these people keep coming back. If this does not work, by and large I will consider my life to have been a failure. I've been saying we can do something other people say can't be done, and if it turns out it can't be done, then I lied, I failed, and in the end, all people will say was that he was nothing but a silver-tongued devil, that he was better at raising money than at executing."

Gary stopped himself short—he'd spoken his worst fear—and as it often did in moments like these, his mind quickly emptied and pivoted, turning to his still-immaterial, still-fantastic PTV. "If we decide to go with a turbo pump, I know we could take it up in six to eight months. A ninety-person company, 50 million a year, twelve to fourteen months, we can have a first functional pump. We need about $120 million, about 60 million we can go sub-orbital. . . ." He spoke frankly, effectively, utterly content now, with unshaken, deep brown eyes.

3

The following Monday, Gary drove down to Mojave again. He gathered his staff in the conference room, informed three-quarters that they'd be jobless as of Friday afternoon, and added that the first "tied-down spin-up" of the Roton ATV would be that Friday morning. Then he left.

Summer had descended once more—the dead coyotes on the roadways, the martial ka-BOOM! of shock waves, the running power in the electric lines sounding like a cooling stream. Brent, Christopher, and Johnny all found themselves soon-to-be unemployed, and the week passed in a fit of depression, aggression, and passive aggression, broken by ecstatic delusory spells of believing that once the ATV spun up its rotors, everything would return to its exalted if hallucinatory state. Gary put the company desks on sale for $25, the bookcases for $10, and Christopher started drinking heavily in his small Mojave apartment, nearly killing his cat by leaving a jar of fiberglassing resin uncapped. Brian played golf daily with Burt Rutan, Brent attended Wicca covens with Dawn. "I like having a girlfriend," Brent declared to me, unabashed. "I like going out at night. I like reading something other than trade journals. I like thinking about things apart from this company and space."

On the Tuesday morning following the layoff announcement,

Brent and I tried to make ourselves feel better by riding bikes up to the flight line, and on our way back, sensing the end, I finally asked him about the pouch he wore around his neck. He stopped, unfastened the cord, and poured into his hand three small stones: rose quartz, tiger's eye, iron pyrite. The stones, he said, were to remind him that people were worth talking to, and to explain he told a story that was simple and hopeful and sad. Brent said he'd stayed on at Caltech after he'd graduated because he wasn't sure what he wanted to do with his life, so he thought he'd audit some classes. But the classes quickly bored him, and he felt profoundly empty, having long ago shunted aside people for sustenance, subsisting on ideas instead. Then, shortly before he left school, he met a girl who delighted him—in Brent's words, "she seemed worth talking to"—and deducing that the same must be true for other humans, he bought a futon and laid it in the back of his pickup and set out on a road trip with the expressed purpose of talking to people, most of whom, he realized, would not even be intellectuals.

Just before his departure, the girl had given him the stones.

I asked Brent if they were working. Clearly they were.

"People are the most interesting problem," he said. "People are the most nonlinear."

On Wednesday, the headline in *The Antelope Valley News* read "Rotary Rocket Wins $900 Million in Contracts," and when Marti finally tracked Gary down at a space conference in Houston—from which Gary planned to fly to Alabama, missing the test on Friday—Gary said, "Those are Swiss cheese contracts. They mean nothing. They're full of holes." (Rotary had issued the press release about the story. The $900 million was to come in part from an unfunded fledgling Arizona company that wanted to establish a commercial base on the moon.) Thursday, Johnny Hernandez distilled yet more peroxide. Because the 80 percent peroxide needed for the ATV's tip rockets—as opposed to the 3 percent peroxide you buy in drugstores—was extremely volatile in heat, he worked at night.

"Fucking wild kingdom out here," he enthused. "Bugs everywhere, look at that snake poop!" The peroxide concentrator hummed in a long, white shed, vents and valves protruding like branch stumps. Johnny wore new wire-rimmed glasses and he'd bleached his hair white, a kind of visual pun. With just one fully staffed day of the company left, some of the test stands had already been partially dismantled, giving the site the appearance of a prematurely old man. Johnny poured some peroxide down a platter-size ant hole and handed me a wedding invitation. "She cried and everything," he said, proud. "You think that means she don't want me to be her old man?"

We kicked around the idea of Johnny applying for a job with Beal Aerospace, a private company in Texas trying to build the largest unmanned commercial rocket in history, but he laughed it off defensively, saying, "But you know what they do with brown people like me down there." He dribbled peroxide on his new leather boots. "If I had my Harley running, I'd be happy flipping burgers. I'd be happy doing anything. I was heartbroken when Gary laid us off—heartbroken. I don't know what I'm going to do after this job. I'm spoiled. I don't want to do nothing else. I might stick around here and just make fuel."

The following morning, Friday, May 21, 1999, everyone met at the high bay at 5:00 A.M., the air blowing gently through the magnificent doors, the desert smelling of sage and scat. The ATV crew cabin now had round emergency exits shaped like human heads, and small arrows pointing to the Plexiglas portal instructing PULL HERE TO CLOSE. Brian and Marti paced separately in their bright orange flight suits and black combat boots, Brian sipping coffee, Marti eating manically—a bagel, a banana, a Moon Pie, cookies, and corn flakes right out of the box. Due to Gary's abrupt change in schedule, no one had had time to test the rotor systems as thoroughly on the whirl stand as the pilots might have hoped. Today's objective was an "all-up-round test"—a test of all of the vehicle's subsystems, including electrical, propellant flow, rotor controls, and crew cabin displays.

High on the yellow arm of the Condor lift, a mechanic duct-taped a small hole in the ATV's igloo crown, lowering himself only when Johnny activated the wheel jacks and began to lever the vehicle up. "Doesn't that thing look good?" Brian asked, partially convincing himself. The Caterpillar tugged the ATV out of the high bay and Brian followed the cone down the runway in his aging Honda Civic, wearing a crisp white T-shirt under his flight suit, Marti in the passenger seat wearing the same blue and white button-down he'd been living in all week. Both carried helmet bags that looked as if they were designed for bowling balls. Families, neighbors, and airport workers bunched behind the fence. "We've got half of Mojave here," Marti grumbled, annoyed, noticing that a handful of truckers had pulled their rigs off the highway. Brian parked on a patch of pavement called the hammerhead. The Roton towered, irresistible, in the flawless desert light.

After the crew chained the vehicle to anchors set in the concrete ramp, a red and yellow fire truck hosed down the tarmac, drawing a circle of water that shone like a skating rink and smelled like spring. Marti and Brian climbed up the spaceship's ladder and the Scaled crew chief followed, securing the round portal door, then jumping back down. The air hung motionless, eerily silent except for the cars, until the rotors spun to life, producing a beat like a high school tuba section, a syncopated *thwump, thwump, thwump.* According to Burt Rutan, the ATV sounded "almost biologic," burning up a thousand pounds of peroxide per minute, quickly draining its 4,000-pound supply. But within seconds one could hear that something was horribly wrong. The rotors were thumping faster and faster, the centripetal force building on itself. Four of the eight ground chains pulled loose from the runway. A piece of plumbing shot out from one of the rotors, landing in a gnarled lump 500 feet due west.

"They took off, man, they took off!" Christopher shouted, leaping off the hood of his truck, unaccountably happy despite the disaster, pressing his palms against his cheeks. "Did you see that? That's awesome! They were probably thinking, 'Oh crap! We're moving!' "

The test lasted less than twenty seconds. Marti and Brian remained in the crew cabin while the rotors wound to a halt and a Scaled engineer trotted out into the scrub to retrieve the wayward pipe. It had hit the mat in an ugly tangle, one end purple, as if bloodied, stained with sodium permanganate. Still, everyone drank the champagne that Gary had provided, performing the gestures of success. "I think it's trying to tell us something," Brian said, squinting into the sun. "I think it's saying it's ready to go, we're ready to fly."

Later that morning, in Building 1, Marti determined that the

ATV had sustained $20,000 worth of damage, and would take six weeks to repair. He tried to reach Gary on his cell phone in Alabama to see if such resources were available. But Gary failed to answer the call after a half dozen tries. An official recording finally announced that the user's messaging service was down.

The layoff party that night was at James's house, a two-bedroom ranch on the airport side of town. James, all of twenty, until that morning a Rotary Rocket machinist, stood thick-bellied and glassy-eyed in the kitchen. Several guys in the living room played a computer game called Frogger, and Johnny, with no glasses and no shirt, rolled dice in the garage. The town felt deflated and hopeless—the flimsy houses, the uncleaned pools, the birds hooting like dogs. Christopher showed up with several M-80s and a twelve-pack of beer. At dusk, Johnny and his tweaker crowd pushed out toward the pool, trailing behind them a tape deck blasting the Beastie Boys anthem "I think I'm losing my mind this time, this time I'm losing my mind."

While Johnny's sturdy and six-foot-tall fiancée Faydra swam in her bikini, Christopher lit off overpowered fireworks, which nobody bothered to watch. James drained a bottle of Yukon Jack and passed out by the toolshed. Johnny smashed a beer can against a Mormon co-worker's head. "Doyle," he said, "you know how it is. You go in for another tattoo, and you come out with a pierced dick."

Later that night we all walked over to Christopher's, ostensibly to drive to Palmdale to drink some more. But everyone just sat in the driveway waiting for the energy to move, while Christopher ran out juggling mason jars, filling the night air with bright green and raspberry red. "You know what that was?" he yelled. "That was barium and strontium and silver with a little sodium." His arms and legs flailed, unhinged, as he sprinted, trailing fuses in the trash-filled wind.

The blacktop felt very hot compared to the cool night air. Rotary's twenty-five-year-old South African aerodynamicist laid himself on the pavement, bracing his head in his hands. "I'm the aerodynamicist! I can't believe I'm the fucking aerodynamicist! You can't just hire a guy right out of school. It's ludicrous, man." We abandoned our plan to drive to Palmdale, and considered drinking over at the high bay. But nobody ever moved—there seemed no point—and to the ignored sounds of Christopher's bombs, we stared at the stars instead.

4

Now only a dozen Rotary employees remained—Marti, Brian, Johnny (saved at the last minute to distill more peroxide), Gary's loyal veteran crew—the whole lot perched unsteadily, as if on a dunking seat, waiting for Gary to pull the lever and splash their heads down. And he tipped the seat on July 17, driving to Mojave and laying off his remaining staff. He imposed the same conflicted schedule as before—test Friday morning, doors locked Friday afternoon.

The day after that announcement, swathed in the Mojave heat, Gary leaned against the former secretary's empty desk, the lobby cluttered with tripods and boom mikes, a BBC crew having previously bought into Gary's vision and now finding themselves in the desert at this inopportune time to film. He stared out through the glass doors, regret welling in the hollows beneath his eyes. "You know what they say in California—three strikes and you're out, three strikes and they throw you in jail." He glanced at the cameras to make sure they were not yet rolling. "And as we all know, I've been through this at least three times before."

The back wall of the lobby remained papered with children's Roton drawings, triangle spaceships capped with circles of rotors, drawn in wobbly crayon. Once the shoot began, Gary composed himself, plowing through his standard effective lines: "Bevin conceived the Roton concept while looking up at a ceiling fan on a honeymoon in Tahiti." "The biggest technical challenge is raising $150 million." "I think I owe, or can blame, most of my life on the Englishman responsible for writing *Profiles of the Future.*" But once the cameraman asked, "What did you tell your staff when you laid them off?" he cracked and began to fall off the script.

"Ultimately," Gary said, "you say, 'I'm sorry for getting you into all this.' You get to an age where what might have been an obsession or a dream just becomes hard work. We have a train wreck converging on Friday. I can't do anything more at this point other than say, 'Sorry, it's been an honor and a privilege.'"

"But you're going to pursue more money, are you not?"

"Sooner or later you reach the bottom."

"Isn't there anything you could do? A public offering to raise more money? It's really an amazing project, I'm sure people would invest."

Gary blushed, enlivened by his interviewer's excitement. "I probably could raise the money," he allowed himself, relieved, "but no investment bank would stand up for it."

NASA, too, came to call that week, two functionaries whom Gary welcomed antically, saying, "You will occasionally hear rumors about layoffs, and rumors that I say bad things about NASA, but publicly I say nice things about administrator Goldin every chance I get." NASA labored under a mandate to develop partnerships with small businesses, so the agents listened to Gary gloss his ATV, his STV, and his two PTVs, but after twenty minutes, the more senior of the civil servants interrupted with irritation. "I have a few questions, a few questions in particular which I'd like to address. First, I'm unclear on what your engine is, and that's the most technically challenging and high-budget item. Also, I've talked to some guys at Marshall, and they say your concept just won't work."

Gary responded with his salesman's nonchalance—we'll give you a new engine, a new concept, anything you want—and the meeting ended preposterously, with NASA offering Gary use of the NASA Ames Research Center and a Memorandum of Understanding agreeing that once the Roton became functional, NASA would consider using it as crew transport to the International Space Station. In return, Gary escorted the agents over to the high bay to sit in the ATV. "The Washington guys are never the same after you bring them out here and let them sit in the vehicle," Gary said privately as we drove the quarter-mile, the agents following in their own car. They flew and crashed the simulator four times each.

"You know the secret of making a small fortune in space?" Gary joked, waving them off. "Start with a large one."

Several unmitigated concerns remained before the hover test. The FAA had never delivered the ATV's Airworthiness Certificate. The vehicle might swing like a pendulum. The rotors might die and the airframe slam down, causing the peroxide tanks to explode. To prepare, Marti and Brian spent the week checking for crew cabin leaks (boosting the scuba pressure, painting dish soap around the door jamb and watching for bubbles), and placing witness blocks atop the gear shafts (small pieces of balsa, the indentations on which reveal how softly or how violently a helicopter lands). On Thursday, the day before the test, while Marti napped at White's and Brian visited his priest, Gary stole a few minutes alone in the crew cabin, heart closed to the tortuous realities.

"I actually don't have any feelings right now," he reported. "Or actually I have the feeling I had after the Percheron blew up—let's clean it all up and do it again. The difference is, I'm not actually that involved in building this thing. I really have nothing to do with it. If I realized it was going to get this complicated I would have killed the project a while ago."

On the ground, Johnny, dressed in a rubber apron and wrap-around sunglasses, checked the fuel filling system, arms folded high across his chest as if he might leap into a Russian kick dance. "Golly gee, she sure is pretty," he called up to his boss.

"She's an ugly little spinster," Gary grumbled, "is what she is."

If Gary was emotionally and professionally severed from the ATV, why was he in the cockpit? No answer, face slack, he fingered the collective stick, struggling toward a better logic for himself. "What I'm really working on these days is a new engine. It can't fail—I know all there is to know already, there's virtually no risk of anything going wrong. We know about regeneratively cooled LOX engines, we know the price of chambers." He looked like a boy caught up in a tree house, spouting fancy words, simultaneously trapped and free. "And I've got another idea up my sleeve. I've now decided to not do an orbital vehicle, but just a little, sub-orbital X vehicle demonstrator—three people to a hundred kilometers, a bulletproof little vehicle. I'm just going to do it for Hollywood, as a marketing ploy. Might even be mono-propellant. Two years, $30 million. . . . We'll paint it up to look like a can of Bud! We'll paint it up to look like a can of Coke! A billion people will see it on CNN. Even if it crashes, they'll get more name exposure because it'll be seen more times. People in L.A. live and die on that kind of thing. We'll paint it up any way you want! Anything you want you can have! It'll be a very straightforward mission—straight up and down. But after that we will have flown men into space, and once you achieve something of that caliber, any number of doors open."

Fuel pumps clicking, Gary fell silent until Brian returned from confessional, the wind holding open the high bay door. "People out there are saying, 'That's Hudson. He's a fraud.' But I dare you to find a single investor who will say that." Gary blinked as Brian approached the spaceship, his mind restively flitting around tomorrow's flight. "How can an officer send troops into battle? You send three guys out scouting knowing that one or more are going to get killed. How can you do that and still stay human?"

Unfortunately for Gary, that week Walt also sent an emissary to Mojave, a handsome twenty-three-year-old Argentinean-European Harvard Business School student named Gustavo. Slim-chested, with a buoyant stride, he planned to become a space entrepreneur, or else sell school sweatshirts at European universities—he'd noticed they sold well in the U.S. In a vacant corner of Building 1, he set himself up as if he were a consultant, drawing diagrams and matrixes intended to save Rotary, including "How to Get to Space/Money/Grace" and "The Investor's Mind."

"You have to challenge the psychology, physiology, and anatomy of an organization," Gustavo explained in his exquisitely refined accent. He was mercifully oblivious to his own naïveté. "I think we should restructure according to this model here." He pointed to a clustered list of all the remaining employees' names, Marti's in thick block letters at the top. "This is the model NASA used during the Apollo project—very fluid, project-based. So Marti is very competent, no? Marti should be the leader. He should stay here every night, not keep flying all over the state. Just check into White's and hold regular meetings, at five A.M. and five P.M. every single day."

Rotary Rocket's official organization chart resembled an incestuous family tree, kinked and crooked, full of knotted personal secrets with several names in multiple spots. Gustavo brought the chart over to Christopher's house one evening, where a bunch of laid-off engineers drank beers and played the computer game You Don't Know Jack. "The problem is, mate," the South African aerodynamicist offered, reaching across the chemical mess, "that this guy here"—he meant Gary, president and CEO—"is running a family instead of a company." Gustavo flipped open his notebook and dutifully wrote this down. A few minutes later he stepped out on the sidewalk. He ducked around the corner to call Walt, pronouncing the ATV "dangerous, far too dangerous to fly."

Before dawn on Friday, July 23, the day of the flight test, Marti informed the BBC camera crew, "I feel ninety-five percent curiosity, five percent fear." Johnny groaned, "I had the worst dream last night. I couldn't find it, I couldn't find the launch pad . . ." and Brian, telegenic, stretched his calves, awaiting the two agents from the FAA. The rest of the crew claimed to have slept "like a baby," "only rolled over when the dogs barked," "right up until the alarm clock rang." At 5:45 A.M., a Cadillac arrived with the Roton's long-awaited Airworthiness Certificate. At six, Gary still nowhere in sight, Brian climbed a few risers up the purple-draped flight stairs, steady as always, legs wide.

"Many of you are probably still half-asleep," he said, sharp in his boots and flight suit, unfolding his prepared speech, "but I'd like to point out to you what a defining moment this is for all of us. Many of you have lamented the fact that our future beyond this morning's endeavor is cloudy, to put it in polite terms, and, frankly, there's not much of a chance in hell that this flight is going to tickle anybody's fancy. But those who want to hold on to a needle-thin strand of hope should come join me, because I'd like to bring your attention to the other side of the coin. I'm standing in front of a sixty-five-foot landing demonstrator of the first innovative rocket design to come along in thirty years. And we're here today to commence flight testing. For many of you, it will be a non-event, but for Marti and me it will be the longest five minutes we've ever endured. It doesn't get much more exciting than this in life."

Brian scanned the high bay—still no Gary. "Clearly, Gary is a little bit sleepy this morning, and he's not with us. He's had this mission and this vision for thirty-plus years, and apparently he's getting a little old. But in his absence, I'd like to declare victory. Many of you will think it's too early, but I take 'em as I see them. Just fifteen minutes ago we were the Rotary Rocket renegades. Now, thanks to a lot of last-minute hustling and arm-twisting of the FAA, we are the proud owners of an Airworthiness Certificate."

In the crowd at the back of the high bay stood Brian's trim wife and three poised kids, enveloped in a sizable gang of past and present Rotary employees. "There's an Ultralight flying this morning—that's a good omen. If all goes well, we should be back in the barn by oh-eight-hundred hours, and tell our stories of success or woe thereafter. It was almost thirty years ago to the day that Neil Armstrong stepped on the moon, so we step forward to champion this vehicle—one of the first manned rockets designed in the past twenty-five years—to push further down that rocky road of progress that Gary and Rotary Rocket have inspired." Just before Brian concluded, Gary entered sheepishly, taking a place far off to the side. "There will be champagne and water at the hold shortly after the flight. Good luck to all of you. Let's go execute."

Gary then spoke briefly, remaining where he was. "I've got just a few words before we send Marti and Brian up. Can I get some theme music? To our future this means very little. To our self-esteem, it means a great deal."

Brian again drove Marti out to the hammerhead, bowling ball helmet bags in the back seat of the Civic, the gray and white cone filling half the windshield, glinting against the sand. Despite efforts at secrecy both intentional and idiosyncratic, several hundred spectators had gathered, including Roger White and most of the Denny's staff. Marti eyeballed the rescue squad. "We've got every free truck in Mojave out here, Christ." He grabbed his Gatorade and his helmet bag, and walked alone over to the ATV.

The plan if something went wrong was for the pilots either to find a way to egress without going through the peroxide, or to pull up on the collective, fly the vehicle to 2,000 feet, arm their parachutes, and eject. "I guess I'm about as scared as I was on my first carrier landing," Brian allowed, still sitting in the driver's seat, clutching the wheel of his car. "More scared than I was the first time I jumped out of a plane. The first time I jumped out of a plane, I wasn't scared. The second time, I was scared. After that, I didn't think I wanted to jump out of perfectly good airplanes anymore."

Along the fence you could pick out the small faces of his family—Brian's older son, off to college in the fall; his younger son, who'd made him the LEGO Roton; his angelic daughter, dressed in a blue-and-white gingham dress matching her mother's; his wife, who'd stayed in a different room last night so as not to disturb his sleep. "Just in case," he said to me, focused and clipped, "I'm giving you my wallet. They won't need it—they'll have a nice life insurance policy." He stepped outside, tapping the door behind him. "The keys are in the side pocket of the car."

The day felt strangely lovely, peaceful, sunny, not yet hot. On the tarmac, Marti rigged a makeshift altimeter while Brian peeled off the orange REMOVE BEFORE FLIGHT flags and slowly circled the vehicle, hands by his sides, posture rod-straight. "I've had this bet with a space shuttle commander friend of mine," he said, breaking out some Yeager-like charm for the BBC, "about who would be the first to launch. He just took off yesterday morning from Cape Canaveral, so now I'm hoping to call it a draw on a technicality: I should be the first guy back down."

A fire truck hosed off the runway. Marti ducked aside to cell-phone his absent wife. Mojave smelled fresh and new for about ten minutes. The pilots then ascended their shining white rocket, leaving the spectators desolate on the ground.

Along with Christopher and the aerodynamicist, I paced a few hundred yards into the burro bush, the sand underfoot feeling as porous as a dried sponge. The aerodynamicist unfolded a tripod and rigged a small video camera. "This is too much responsibility," he said, positioning the lens. "If I mess this up I'm fired."

"You're fired anyway," Christopher said.

"That's right, dude man, I forgot. Hey, did somebody tell Marti not to go to orbit?"

After thirty minutes of waiting, the rotors still motionless, Christopher cracked. "The worst thing that could happen is that we could snap a water line, and Marti and Brian'd be overboiled chickens in a stew pot in a matter of minutes. But I guess if the kerosene caught fire, it'd burn 'em to death just the same." Another half-hour later, the fire truck hosed down the tarmac again, and an hour after that the rotors finally spun up. Marti revved the engine and then backed off, sitting on the pad for over a minute, what felt like a very long time. Later we would all learn that the data acquisition system, or DAS, failed shortly after the spin up, and the throttle over-speed "pusher"—a mechanical device installed after the last test to push the stick down, keeping the RPM low—pushed the stick down too strongly, making it difficult for the pilots to generate sufficient rotor speed. But eventually the cone did lift up, rocking back off its gear and climbing dreamily, as if in slow motion, five stately feet, until, due to low RPM, the gigantic cone and its halo of blades descended back down.

In order to climb again, Marti had to lower the collective and quickly raise it again, pumping the energy stored in the rotors to jump the ATV into the air. Thus the cone rose a second time, languidly, liquidly, in its almost romantic fashion, ethereal and yet heavy, as if lost in sleep. Each time the ATV set down and lifted up again it floated slightly higher, burning peroxide at the rate of a jet in full afterburner, losing 1,300 pounds between one bounce and the next. On its second hop, horribly, the cone lifted up off-center and began a pendulum swing, its four landing gears oscillating from side to side, like feet under a hammock, widening instead of dampening its arc. On the third hop the cone not only teetered laterally but rotated clockwise and drifted to the left. After that Marti set the helicopter down. The right gear hit the tarmac, then the cone rolled left.

And still the spraying champagne, the BBC celebrity, the compromised but heartfelt declarations of victory. Once down on the ground, Brian spun his wife around in a circle, her gingham dress twirling like a pinwheel, along with her straight black hair. "Sorry," he said, kissing her on the forehead, "you're not going to be rich after all, baby."

Marti addressed the television cameras. "If you use rocket test standards, that was a huge success. Either it blows up or it doesn't. And we didn't even break the thing."

The crew spent the remainder of the morning watching flight videos—shot from the north, from the west, inside the crew cabin—until the precipitous cone took on a comfortable certainty, like the overplayed footage of the collapsing Tacoma Narrows Bridge. Near lunchtime, Anne Hudson pulled me aside to teach me the basics of Jin Shin Jitsu, a discipline she'd been studying since the first round of layoffs, when she left her Rotary Rocket job. She flattened my hand in hers, smoothing open my tense palm. "Pulling on the thumb alleviates worry," she said. "Pulling on the index finger calms fear. The middle finger is for anger. The ring finger is for grief." She lingered on my pinkie for ten or twenty seconds. "The pinkie," she said, "eliminates pretense. You know, when outside you're laughing but you're crying inside?"

5

The morning after the hover I drove back to the high bay to find Johnny chainsawing apart the sea-green foam and carbon fiber carcasses, the tooling for the ATV. The American flag, long draped on the back wall, had finally come down, and the rocket dangled from the crane on the ceiling, spent and swinging slightly, like a newly hanged man. On the great yellow arm of the Condor hoist, a mechanic floated beside the igloo, removing the rotors from the giant cone and packing them away in the coffin-like boxes in which they'd first arrived. Gary had announced bargain prices for all his assets, so strangers rifled through cabinets and tool benches, bidding on the large equipment, particularly the hydraulic mule. Nothing here held any real value—the fittings were too big, the high bay too big, who needed a rotary engine pit? "Damn vultures," Johnny muttered, a leg slung over the payload bay molding, as he sawed three cuts lengthwise, three cuts widthwise into the black and green Styrofoam. The sky outside had turned flat blue. Johnny forklifted the massive shards into a waiting dumpster. "It's hotter than shit out here," he said, and sprayed himself down with water.

That afternoon, I dropped by Building 1 to say goodbye to Gary, and found Anne sitting cross-legged, nearly slaphappy, on the floor of his office, her husband hunched behind his desk, his left thumb pressed into the cup above his temple, right hand still on the phone. The lines of his face rearranged themselves at an alarming rate. "Yesterday afternoon," he said, after a bizarre and extended silence, "I FedExed Walt a video of the test, and I just hung up." His mouth gaped open involuntarily. "Walt says he still wants to fund the flight test program. He mentioned a few million for the down-the-runway and up-and-over tests. I basically told him I didn't think it was a good idea, but the vehicle's intact, and the building's intact, and so I'm putting the rotor blades back on."

A small crew mustered the courage to believe again, but a month later, in late August, Gary announced to me his intention to resign. He had closed his grand office in Redwood Shores, and I found him in his townhouse garage, staring at the maple scraps from a hardwood floor he'd installed the last time he was unemployed. Behind the cutting table, boxes rose from floor to ceiling, files Anne had packed away from each of her husband's previous companies, many not marked or labeled. "I never intend to open any of the boxes anyway," Gary explained, his voice brittle. He wore a green Hawaiian shirt dotted with pink hibiscus flowers. "I'm like Arthur C. Clarke, remember? Don't care much about the past, or about the present either. I only care about the future."

The house looked unchanged in the four months since I'd been there—the childhood space books in their glass-shuttered cabinets, the science fiction paintings on the clean white walls. The only notable addition was the GARY HUDSON, CEO, ROTARY ROCKET placard placed atop the large-screen TV. Gary had filched the nametag from a lunch he'd recently attended at

NASA. He'd been seated next to NASA chief Dan Goldin—proof, or so Gary had chosen to believe, that Gary was more than just a silver-tongued devil.

Steering his BMW past the matching condos and wet, manicured lawns, Gary confessed he wanted to resign because of a bad teleconference with Walt. In that conversation, Walt had referred to the RocketJet engine as "a piece of dog meat" and requested that detailed budgets be made for the forthcoming $2 million, with variances against them every two weeks. Gary's eyes spiraled as he tried to remain confident, terrified at the thought of cool-hearted scrutiny, like a young man caught in some serious adult trouble for the first time. "I now understand Richard Nixon," he said. "Just before Nixon resigned he told the press, 'You're not going to have Richard Nixon to kick around anymore.' Walt spent $30 million. I spent three years of my life! Walt can make his money back! Time is an arrow. Those years are gone."

The billboards along the horizon promised effortless, immaterial connection, growth, and progress. "We had a $150-million program. We spent twenty percent of the money. How could we have gotten to the end of the program if we spent nineteen percent of the money? I've finally come to the conclusion that Walt doesn't understand the space business at all. I mentioned to him that Hughes is building satellites for ICO. He'd never even heard of ICO. He doesn't know anything about the space industry, and we've had to play by Walt's rules: *Don't take any government money. Don't accept any government contracts.*" Gary parked amid a clutch of imported roadsters beside a bistro on the bay. "We didn't start from an even playing field, we started in the hole. Nobody could possibly have made this work."

Over composed salads, Gary gradually reined in the grandiosity and backpedaled on his intention to quit. First he said, "Even if Walt set aside $100 million dollars I probably wouldn't take it." Then, "I'd most likely take the money, but what I'd do is lock four or five smart guys in a room and order out pizza until they figured out what to do next." His performance resembled one of those early engine tests I'd watched backward and in slow motion, the wild destructive energies re-collecting themselves, the explosion slipping back into the can. Egrets fished and floated along the marshy shoreline, oblivious to the planes pressing down toward SFO. The scene called to mind Delmore Schwartz's brilliantly titled story "In Dreams Begin Responsibilities." "The Roton is probably too much for people to believe in, and maybe too much to do. The most reasonable thing at this juncture would be to just wait five, six, eight years until Walt's fund is worth $3 billion. Then Walt will be able to finance a $250 million project. And that's what really needs to happen here—a single investor needs to put in all the money."

On the way back to his condo, Gary stopped at the post office to pick up his mail. By the time we arrived, he'd talked himself into keeping his job. "Do you think you'll try this again someday?" I asked, preparing to drive away.

"I'd be a liar if I said I didn't want to," he said. "The question is, will anybody let me?"

September cooled into a dizzying month of repositioning the ATV's mirrors, climbing in and out of its hull, fixing the DAS and the over-speed pusher, and charging up the scuba tanks for the translational, or down the runway, flight. In the midst of all this, on September 18, Johnny got married, emerging from the California City Community Church to a line of parked Harleys, Faydra on his arm, curls piled atop her head, white wedding dress stretched over her four-months-pregnant belly. Johnny wore a long coat, wide pants, and a purple vest. His ring blinked with five small diamonds. He had two new piercings in his lip.

The reception immediately followed in Central Park—chicken, ribs, burgers, and spaghetti salad, a DJ playing mismatched music to suit the motley crowd. I spent most of the evening chatting with Victor Foulk, a local Rotary hand, nineteen years old, with raw eyes and a narrow body hidden under baggy clothes. For his emergency contact number he'd listed the obituary desk at *The Antelope Valley News*. He interrupted himself every few minutes to ask why I had not yet walked away. Sunglasses on well past dark, Victor told me his father died when he was seventeen and his mom when he was eighteen, and he married a few years ago and then moved out of the house, and now wasn't allowed to see his three-year-old son because, as he put it, "my ex-wife is a bitch." Perched atop a picnic table we watched girls dance—a tweaker in knee socks, a weathered beauty in tight jeans. Victor said, "I don't like the women you find in Mojave. They're all promiscuous—you can tell just by looking." After the last flight he'd sent Gary this letter:

Gary,

I unfortunately was unable to catch you after the meeting. I don't have much to say, so I will keep it very brief.

In the past two years as a member of this project, I have learned much. I have also performed many technical miracles with scraps and NO budget. I will continue to do so, as long as I am needed, whether you can pay me or not. I live and breathe this dream as much as you do, and I do not ever want to hear that you are giving up. You are the one who has lead *[sic]* us this far, I am not turning back. No matter what it takes, despite all odds and even if only once, WE WILL FLY.

Victor

The following week, Johnny returned to making peroxide, spooking himself in the airplane graveyard, sleeping fitfully in his truck. Early one morning, a Mojave green snake slithered into the distillery. "Green ain't no joke," Johnny reported later back in the high bay. "Sidewinders, I let 'em bite me. But green? It hurts like seven bees, like seven wasps." He'd dripped some peroxide on his tongue. "Makes it feel numb," he said.

The ATV's first real flight, the final test before the terrifying up-and-over mission, took place on October 12, 1999, and at six A.M. both Marti and Brian handed me their wallets and keys. The air felt cool that morning and the two pilots walked wordlessly behind the vehicle, the cone now streaked with purple catalyst, no longer the pure product of one man's imagination, more street-worn, less pristine. The regular crowd bunched behind the fence—Christopher, down from his new job designing nuclear warheads in Silicon Valley; Brent, now living in Santa Rosa with Dawn, had stayed home. Gary arrived at ten to seven, dressed as squarely as a headmaster, in a navy blazer, sport shirt, and striped tie. "Well, have a good flight—don't break it," he said. The pink and tan light off the buttes added color to his face. He walked alone to stand by the tower, near the painted X on the runway that marked the landing spot.

My task was to drive a 1962 GMC truck down the tarmac,

just behind the Roton. Again, unnervingly, the cone wobbled at the start-up, producing its low, thumping heartbeat, that rupturing biologic noise. But once in flight, the vehicle lost its awkwardness, settling into a glorious, if staggering, vision—the world's tallest, largest, and most inefficient helicopter flying through the air, its nose nudged forward fifteen degrees, its tail tucked back. The vehicle glided dreamily, patiently, as if in slow motion, like a blown-up Michelin doll, its movements pillowy, almost vague. Nothing could have been more improbable—here in the unaesthetic desert, this stunning first prototype of a civilian spaceship, flying laterally down the runway at a speed of fifty-three miles per hour, an altitude of seventy-five feet. The aging GMC truck could not keep up. I lagged well behind the yaw thrusters as Marti set the cone down atop the X, having transported Gary's dream 4,182 feet, under its own power, from one place to another, for the first time. Everyone gathered, hugging, spraying champagne, kissing the spaceship, the ground, each other, snapping pictures in the sun and wind. Gary stood back, frozen, catatonic. "Damned incredible," he said to all who approached. "Damned incredible. Must have cut my life short by a year or two."

Gary left immediately, and that was the last time I saw him in Mojave. The two pilots wanted to fly the "up-and-over mission"—take the ATV to 2,000 feet, kill the power to the rotors, then auto-rotate down—and at first Gary agreed, with the caveat, "they'll just have to find the appropriate drugs to sedate me." But a month later, just a week before the flight, he laid off the remaining staff and scrubbed the program for good. He said he couldn't see the test bringing in new investment money, and so he couldn't in good conscience risk two men's lives. Lost on nobody was the fact that Rotary still had a million dollars in the bank—a nice cushion on which Gary could fly around to space conferences and symposia, screening his Roton video, working his silvery tongue.

Officially, Gary planned to use the million dollars to produce preliminary drawings for his next rocket, the PTV-1, a vehicle much heavier and more complicated than the ATV—it'd even have a rocket engine—one he claimed would be better suited for testing the Roton's approach and landing system, even though he'd built the ATV specifically for that purpose and thus far it had worked fine. Neither Brian nor Marti could find any peace. Brian had turned down a job at the International Test Pilot School in London because he wanted to see the flight test program to the end. Now, in pleated khakis and a blue fleece jacket zipped to the collar, he jerked about his office, removing his Desert Storm and F-18 patches from his wall, sticking the pins back into the corkboard hard. "You got a secret you're not telling us?" he sneered, tight-jawed, as if speaking to Gary. "You got a plan for that million dollars?" He slid his LEGO crew cabin off his bookshelf. He bobbled the plastic in his hand, then, disgusted, tore it apart.

"There are guys, seagulls, who train to be carrier pilots and then get out there and start flapping and saying, 'No way, I'm not doing that, I'm not landing on that thing.' Same thing with crossing the beach. You sign up saying, 'I'm going to support and defend the Constitution,' and when the shooting starts, you say 'I'm not up to this.' In my mind, this is the same. This program had a flight test component. There needed to be flight tests. If Gary didn't have the stomach for it, he shouldn't have gotten involved in the first place. You can't be saying you have all these grand plans and visions if you're not willing to step up to the plate. If you don't have the disposition for it, you shouldn't be taking people's money in the first place."

Separately, over in the high bay, Marti had locked himself in the crew cabin, also screaming at Gary in his head. The entire vehicle felt like an exhibit in a science museum, a grand toy built overlarge and simple to make a viewer feel full of wonder, small. Strangely, the American flag hung once again on the back wall, the red, white, and blue stunning against the purple-painted girders, the whole tableau unaccountably beautiful, the white of the Roton against the yellow of the Condor, the swirling red spiral of the Rotary logo, the earth painted green and blue. Marti had installed a new wind vane just outside the portal door, black and white and silver, like a Miró drawing, with its elegant, complicated lines. "You know what you should call your book?" he said to me, infuriated but, despite himself, still bemused, unable, as we all were, to muster real contempt. "*The Doer and the Dreamer.* I'm a doer and Gary's a dreamer. And I don't just like to do, I like to win. It's the Navy way—I like to cream the other guy. And what we've got here is un-American. It's fourth down and inches with ten seconds left. That's the ball game, that's it, and Gary's quit, gone home, punted to the other team."

A sonic boom shook the high bay but Marti told me not to bother running to look outside—the plane had flown straight up. "You know what the statistics on helicopter tests are? Helicopter test casualties are one per hundred thousand. In rockets, they're one per hundred, which means rockets are a thousand times more dangerous. How were these guys ever going to test a rocket if they weren't even willing to test a helicopter? It doesn't make any sense. All we needed was one more flight."

Marti shook his head. The end had come, and everybody was too spent, too sated, too exposed to themselves for it; too threatened by self-knowledge to relish catching Gary out on his dream. "I'm a guy who never quits anything," Marti continued, his feet compulsively working the pedals, his hands gripping the collective control. "Gary is a guy who dreams of things and who starts things I would never start." Is this why we had all come here? The question hung in the air. Marti phoned his wife to say he'd be spending the night at White's. The ATV never left the ground again, but the rotors still fluttered when you worked the stick, so Marti shut the door of that spectacular delusion and cocooned himself inside.

ACKNOWLEDGMENTS

Let me first and very sincerely thank Gary Hudson and his wife, Anne, both of whom have been unfailingly warm, kind, and available to me throughout all the reporting and life that transpired while I was writing this book.

Marti Sarigul-Klijn and Brian Binnie were also exceptionally patient and generous with both their time and expertise.

Also—please bear the indulgence—I need to thank everybody who worked at Rotary Rocket (apologies if this list omits anyone): Paul Allision, Bill Anderson, Bart Bakker, Richard Bielawa, Jeff Blattell, Nelson Brazeau, Tom Brosz, Mary Lou Cabbett, Richard Caselli, Phil Chapman, Mark Comninos, Mary Contreras, Richard Corbett, Dan Delong, Karen Donohue, Ken Doyle, Brent Eubanks, Harry Ferguson, Victor Foulk, Michele Galmiche, Rick Giarusso, Jeff Greason, Jim Grote, Helena Hardman, Duane Hare, Roger Hensley, Johnny Hernandez, Emily Hogge, Roger Houghton, Mark Hovaten, Geoffery Hughes, Richard Hurwitz, Mike Iribe, Aleta Jackson, Felipe Jimenez, Kristen Johnson, Doug Jones, Michel Kamel, Becki Kenngott, Aaron Kushner, William (Buzz) Lange, Jake Lapota, James Laughlin, Michael Laughlin, Andre Lavoie, Cindy Lee, Neil Macphee, Tony Martin, Daniel Means, Bevin McKinney, Roman Nenadovic, John Nezits, David Nixon, Beatrice Oceguera, Tom

Pavia, Patricia Prado, Jim Reinhart, Geri Rice, Sean Robinson, Andrea Saint Germain, Joe Shelton, Rand Simberg, Christopher Smith, Richard Stockmans, Terry Van Blaricom, Pam Wagner, and Heayoon Woo. I have always been a cynic drawn to believers, and I feel honored that you opened your lives to me, and looked out for me, when necessary, in Mojave.

In the space world, a place in which I needed much education, Walt Anderson, Mitch Clapp, Peter Diamandis, David Gump, Max Hunter, Chirinjeev Kathuria, Mike Kelly, Charles Lurio, Jeffery Manber, Bob Morgan, Richard Smithies, Rick Tumlinson, Henry Vanderbilt, and Robert Zubrin all made themselves available beyond the call. Roger White and his family gave me a home in the desert. Shane DuBow, David Kestenbaum, Anton Krukowski, Apollinaire Scherr, and Alix Spiegel were all incredible friends and invaluable readers, all of whom I hope to repay someday. My brother, David Weil, sent me a check so I could write the proposal for this book—thank you. Kris Dahl turned that proposal into a book contract, and Ann Harris edited that book with care. My husband, Dan Duane—a tremendous writer and editor—was attentive in every way throughout. And I required a lot of attention. I am very grateful.